SLOW COOKER RECIPES

by
Jean Paré

companyscoming.com
visit our web-site

Dedication

For busy households everywhere—
ready when you are!

Props Courtesy Of: Creations By Design; Le Gnome;
Scona Clayworks; Stokes; The Basket House

SLOW COOKER RECIPES

Thirty-sixth Printing March 2004

Canadian Cataloguing in Publication Data

Paré, Jean
Slow cooker recipes

Includes index.
ISBN 1-895455-37-5

1. Electric cookery, Slow. I. Title.

TX827.P372 1998   641.5'884   C98-900461-9

Published and Distributed by
Company's Coming Publishing Limited
2311 – 96 Street
Edmonton, Alberta, Canada T6N 1G3
www.companyscoming.com

**Published Simultaneously in
Canada and the United States of America**

Printed In Canada

Company's Coming Cookbook Series

Quick & easy recipes, everyday ingredients!

Original Series

- Softcover, 160 pages
- 6" x 9" (15 cm x 23 cm) format
- Lay-flat binding
- Full colour photos
- Nutrition information

Greatest Hits Series

- Softcover, 106 & 124 pages
- 8" x 9 9/16" (20 cm x 24 cm) format
- Paperback binding
- Full colour photos
- Nutrition information

Lifestyle Series

- Softcover, 160 pages
- 8" x 10" (20 cm x 25 cm) format
- Paperback & spiral binding
- Full colour photos
- Nutrition information

Special Occasion Series

- Hardcover & softcover, 192 pages
- 8 1/2" x 11" (22 cm x 28 cm) format
- Durable sewn binding
- Full colour throughout
- Nutrition information

See page 157
for a complete listing
of _all_ cookbooks
or visit
companyscoming.com

table of Contents

the Jean Paré story

Jean Paré grew up understanding that the combination of family, friends and home cooking is the essence of a good life. From her mother she learned to appreciate good cooking, while her father praised even her earliest attempts. When she left home she took with her many acquired family recipes, her love of cooking and her intriguing desire to read recipe books like novels!

In 1963, when her four children had all reached school age, Jean volunteered to cater to the 50th anniversary of the Vermilion School of Agriculture, now Lakeland College. Working out of her home, Jean prepared a dinner for over 1000 people which launched a flourishing catering operation that continued for over eighteen years. During that time she was provided with countless opportunities to test new ideas with immediate feedback—resulting in empty plates and contented customers! Whether preparing cocktail sandwiches for a house party or serving a hot meal for 1500 people, Jean Paré earned a reputation for good food, courteous service and reasonable prices.

"Why don't you write a cookbook?" Time and again, as requests for her recipes mounted, Jean was asked that question. Jean's response was to team up with her son, Grant Lovig, in the fall of 1980 to form Company's Coming Publishing Limited. April 14, 1981, marked the debut of "150 DELICIOUS SQUARES", the first Company's Coming cookbook in what soon would become Canada's most popular cookbook series.

Jean Paré's operation has grown steadily from the early days of working out of a spare bedroom in her home. Full-time staff includes marketing personnel located in major cities across Canada. Home Office is based in Edmonton, Alberta in a modern building constructed specially for the company.

Today the company distributes throughout Canada and the United States in addition to numerous overseas markets, all under the guidance of Jean's daughter, Gail Lovig. Best-sellers many times over, Company's Coming cookbooks are published in English and French, plus a Spanish-language edition is available in Mexico. Familiar and trusted in home kitchens the world over, Company's Coming cookbooks are offered in a variety of formats, including the original softcover series.

Jean Paré's approach to cooking has always called for quick and easy recipes using everyday ingredients. Even when travelling, she is constantly on the lookout for new ideas to share with her readers. At home, she can usually be found researching and writing recipes, or working in the company's test kitchen. Jean continues to gain new supporters by adhering to what she calls "the golden rule of cooking": never share a recipe you wouldn't use yourself. It's an approach that works—*millions of times over!*

Foreword

Imagine entering your home to the aroma of food cooking away in your slow cooker. It's a wonderful feeling, knowing that while you were elsewhere, dinner was progressing nicely at home.

Some of these recipes can be prepared in the morning and left to cook all day—others won't require cooking for quite that long, but can still offer you freedom of time to garden, shop, or run errands.

Slow cookers offer many benefits that most of us aren't aware of. For instance, a slow cooker can also serve as an extra pot anytime you cook; it won't heat up your kitchen, and, unlike most other conventional cooking methods, it won't dry out food. Meals can be served right from a slow cooker, but for a more impressive presentation, you may want to place food in a serving bowl and add a few garnishes.

For more tips and information on how to make the best use of your slow cooker, check out pages 8 and 9.

Now it's time to plug in your slow cooker and have some fun. For something to simmer all day, you must try Beef Barley Soup. A quicker dish, like Macaroni And Cheese, will satisfy even the fussiest family member. Amaze everyone that you made Banana Bread in your slow cooker!

Featuring a wide range of recipe ideas to suit practically any occasion, SLOW COOKER RECIPES offers you the chance to take life a little easier.

Jean Paré

Each recipe has been analyzed using the most up-to-date version of the Canadian Nutrient File from Health Canada, which is based on the United States Department of Agriculture (USDA) Nutrient Database. If more than one ingredient is listed (such as "hard margarine or butter"), the first ingredient is used in the analysis. Where an ingredient reads "sprinkle," "optional," or "for garnish," it is not included as part of the nutrition information.

Margaret Ng, B.Sc. (Hon), M.A.
Registered Dietitian

TIPS & HINTS

BEVERAGES: Slow cookers make an excellent warmer for any hot drink. As a general rule, always heat beverages on Low. When ready, simply leave your slow cooker on, ready to serve hot drinks to your guests.

BREADS & CAKES: Slow cookers will successfully cook yeast breads and scratch cakes, but you should expect slightly different results in appearance. For instance, they may or may not dome slightly in the center. Also, because moisture is retained in a slow cooker, both breads and cakes will appear more porous with larger air holes and a slightly coarser texture.

If you would like to warm dinner rolls in your slow cooker, wrap them securely first in foil. Cover and heat on Low for 2 to 3 hours, or on High for 1 to 1½ hours.

DAIRY PRODUCTS: Most dairy products don't tolerate long periods of heat. Add during the last hour of cooking whenever possible. Processed cheese and cheese spreads do better than harder cheeses.

DESSERTS: As a general rule of thumb, most desserts (such as puddings and cakes) are cooked on High. Also, because some dessert recipes call for a pan or dish to be set inside the slow cooker, make sure everything fits before you begin.

MEATS: Less tender cuts of meat work well in a slow cooker. Increased moisture and longer cooking times break down tougher cuts, producing a more tender result. There is also less shrinkage of meat because of the low heat and long cooking duration. A meat thermometer, especially an instant one, is a big help in determining the doneness of meat—but avoid checking it too often, and do it as quickly as you can to prevent loss of heat and moisture. For best results using ground beef, scramble-fry or precook before adding to the slow cooker. Meat should be defrosted before cooking, however for safety reasons we do not recommend that you use your slow cooker to defrost.

PASTA: Pasta should not be included in ingredients that you are assembling the night before, because they tend to become mushy.

PREPARATION: As a convenience to avoiding rushed mornings, most ingredients can be prepared, measured and put into a slow cooker the night before. Note that rice and pasta are an exception to this, and should only be added just before cooking begins. If meat, milk or eggs, are included in the recipe, be sure to place your assembled ingredients in the refrigerator overnight.

RICE: The best form of rice to use in a slow cooker is converted rice, because it is less likely to become too sticky or mushy.

SETTINGS: Most slow cookers use only two settings—Low and High. It is virtually impossible to overcook foods on Low, but overcooking may become a problem on High. For best results, you should develop a "feel" for your slow cooker by keeping track of cooking times that produce the results you want. When cooking on Low, try to avoid removing the lid too often since it takes a long time to build up lost heat and moisture.

SIZES: Regular slow cookers range in size from 3½ qts. to 6 qts, and may or may not have a removable liner. In addition, you may find smaller sizes on the market, about .5 qt. (.5 L). These are primarily used for making dips and sauces, and are an ideal size for serving chocolate or cheese fondue. Each recipe identifies what size of slow cooker was used during testing.

TIMING: All of our recipes (with a few exceptions) give an approximate time for both Low and High settings. If you use a different size of slow cooker than what is listed, keep in mind that it should be at least half full for times and results to be reliable. The actual cooking time of a recipe will also depend on the type of food, the starting temperature of the food, and the size, or various sizes, the food is cut into.

VEGETABLES: Because fresh, raw vegetables take longer to cook than meats, they should be thinly sliced or cut into small pieces and then placed on the bottom of the slow cooker. Frozen or canned vegetables may be added to the top if desired.

SNACK MIX

An easy way to whip up a bowl of munchies. Very addictive!

Hard margarine (or butter)	¼ cup	60 mL
Seasoning salt	1½ tsp.	7 mL
Garlic powder	¼ tsp.	1 mL
Onion powder	¾ tsp.	4 mL
Celery salt	¼ tsp.	1 mL
Grated Parmesan cheese	1 tbsp.	15 mL
Pretzel sticks	1½ cups	375 mL
Salted peanuts	1½ cups	375 mL
O-shaped toasted oat cereal	2 cups	500 mL
Whole wheat cereal squares	2 cups	500 mL

Combine first 6 ingredients in 5 quart (5 L) slow cooker. Cook on High to melt margarine. Turn heat to Low.

Add remaining 4 ingredients. Stir well. Cover. Cook for 3½ hours. Remove cover. Stir. Cook for about 30 minutes, stirring once or twice. Makes 7 cups (1.75 L).

½ cup (125 mL): 194 Calories; 12.5 g Total Fat; 537 mg Sodium; 6 g Protein; 17 g Carbohydrate

Pictured on page 17.

PACIFIC PECANS

Dark colored with good spicy flavor.

Hard margarine (or butter)	2 tbsp.	30 mL
Soy sauce	1 tbsp.	15 mL
Salt	½ tsp.	2 mL
Garlic powder	¼ tsp.	1 mL
Onion powder	¼ tsp.	1 mL
Cayenne pepper	⅛ tsp.	0.5 mL
Pecan halves	2 cups	500 mL

Stir first 6 ingredients in 3½ quart (3.5 L) slow cooker. Cook on High to melt margarine.

Add pecans. Stir well. Reduce heat to Low. Cover. Cook for 1½ hours, stirring at half-time. Turn heat to High. Remove cover. Cook for 20 minutes, stirring twice. Spread on tray to cool. Makes 2 cups (500 mL).

2 tbsp. (30 mL): 106 Calories; 10.8 g Total Fat; 161 mg Sodium; 1 g Protein; 3 g Carbohydrate

Ribs in golden juice. Deliciously sweet and tangy.

White vinegar	½ cup	125 mL
Granulated sugar	1 cup	250 mL
Ketchup	⅔ cup	150 mL
Onion flakes	1 tbsp.	15 mL
Worcestershire sauce	1 tbsp.	15 mL
Water	1 cup	250 mL
Pork spareribs, cut into short lengths and into single rib pieces	3 lbs.	1.4 kg

Place first 6 ingredients in 5 quart (5 L) slow cooker. Stir well.

Add ribs. Stir. Cover. Cook on Low for 10 to 12 hours or on High for 5 to 6 hours. Makes about 37 ribs.

1 rib: 73 Calories; 3.4 g Total Fat; 79 mg Sodium; 4 g Protein; 7 g Carbohydrate

Nice curry flavor. Very good.

Natural almonds with brown skin (1⅓ cups, 325 mL)	½ lb.	225 g
Hard margarine (or butter)	1 tbsp.	15 mL
Salt	¼ tsp.	1 mL
Curry powder	1½ tsp.	7 mL

Place all 4 ingredients in 3½ quart (3.5 L) slow cooker. Cook on High to melt margarine. Stir well. Cover. Cook on Low for about 2 hours. Stir. Turn heat to High. Cook, uncovered, for about 1 hour, stirring at half-time. Spread on tray to cool. Makes 1⅓ cups (325 mL).

2 tbsp. (30 mL): 130 Calories; 11.7 g Total Fat; 76 mg Sodium; 4 g Protein; 4 g Carbohydrate

Pictured on page 17.

SALTED ALMONDS: Simply omit curry powder.

SWEET AND SOUR WINGS

In dark flavorful sauce. These are among the first appetizers to disappear.

Whole chicken wings (or drumettes)	3 lbs.	1.4 kg
Brown sugar, packed	1 cup	250 mL
All-purpose flour	¼ cup	60 mL
Water	½ cup	125 mL
White vinegar	¼ cup	60 mL
Ketchup	1½ tbsp.	25 mL
Soy sauce	¼ cup	60 mL
Garlic powder	¼ tsp.	1 mL
Onion flakes	1 tbsp.	15 mL
Salt	½ tsp.	2 mL
Prepared mustard	½ tsp.	2 mL

Discard tip and cut wings apart at joint. Place chicken pieces in 5 quart (5 L) slow cooker.

Mix brown sugar and flour well in saucepan. Add water, vinegar and ketchup. Stir. Add remaining 5 ingredients. Heat and stir until boiling and thickened. Pour over wings. Cover. Cook on Low for 8 to 9 hours or on High for 4 to 4½ hours until tender. Serve from slow cooker or remove to platter. Makes about 28 wing pieces or about 18 drumettes.

1 wing piece: 99 Calories; 5 g Total Fat; 4.3 mg Sodium; 241 g Protein; 10 g Carbohydrate

Pictured on page 17.

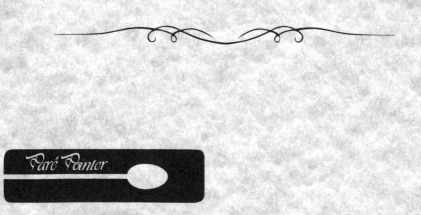

If only you could cross an octopus with a hen, you would get chicken with drumsticks for everyone.

MEXI DIP

When you dip down with a sturdy chip or spoon, you get different layers. Wrecks many a diet. Serve with chips.

Light cream cheese, softened	**2 × 8 oz.**	**2 × 250 g**
Canned flakes of ham, with liquid, mashed together	**6.5 oz.**	**184 g**
Grated medium Cheddar cheese	**3 cups**	**750 mL**
Medium or hot salsa	**½ cup**	**125 mL**
Canned chopped green chilies, drained	**4 oz.**	**114 mL**
Chili powder	**½-1 tsp.**	**2-5 mL**

Mash cream cheese with fork in bowl. Spread in bottom of 3½ quart (3.5 L) slow cooker.

Sprinkle ham evenly over top. Sprinkle with Cheddar cheese.

Stir salsa and green chilies together. Spoon over top.

Sprinkle with chili powder. Cover. Cook on Low for 2 to 2½ hours until quite warm. Do not stir. Makes 4¼ cups (1 L).

1 tbsp. (15 mL): 42 Calories; 3.4 g Total Fat; 173 mg Sodium; 2 g Protein; 1 g Carbohydrate

CLAM DIP

Fairly mild dip, but good. Serve with crackers, chips or chunks of bread.

Light cream cheese, softened	**8 oz.**	**250 g**
Light sour cream	**¼ cup**	**60 mL**
Worcestershire sauce	**1 tbsp.**	**15 mL**
Grated onion	**1 tbsp.**	**15 mL**
Lemon juice	**1 tbsp.**	**15 mL**
Salt	**½ tsp.**	**2 mL**
Garlic powder	**⅛ tsp.**	**0.5 mL**
Canned minced clams, drained	**5 oz.**	**142 g**

Combine first 7 ingredients in bowl. Mix until well blended.

Add clams. Mix. Turn into 3½ quart (3.5 L) slow cooker. Cover. Cook on Low for 1¾ hours, stirring occasionally, until quite warm. Makes 2 cups (500 mL).

1 tbsp. (15 mL): 21 Calories; 1.4 g Total Fat; 121 mg Sodium; 2 g Protein; 1 g Carbohydrate

BEEFY CHIP DIP

Thick, meaty and cheesy. Add more chili powder to suit your taste. Serve with chips.

Lean ground beef	1 lb.	454 g
Grated Monterey Jack cheese (¾ lb., 340 g)	3 cups	750 mL
Worcestershire sauce	2 tsp.	10 mL
Canned chopped green chilies	4 oz.	114 mL
Medium or hot salsa	1 cup	250 mL
Chili powder	½ tsp.	2 mL
Onion powder	½ tsp.	2 mL

Scramble-fry ground beef in non-stick frying pan until no longer pink. Drain. Use fork to mash and break up beef. Turn into 3½ quart (3.5 L) slow cooker.

Add next 6 ingredients. Stir. Cover. Cook on Low for 1¾ to 2 hours, stirring occasionally, until quite warm. Makes 4 cups (1 L).

1 tbsp. (15 mL): 33 Calories; 2.2 g Total Fat; 103 mg Sodium; 3 g Protein; 1 g Carbohydrate

SPINACH DIP

Mild and tasty. Popeye's favorite. Serve with chunks of bread or chips.

Light cream cheese, softened	8 oz.	250 g
Light salad dressing (or mayonnaise)	½ cup	125 mL
Lemon juice	2 tsp.	10 mL
Salt	½ tsp.	2 mL
Garlic powder	⅛ tsp.	0.5 mL
Worcestershire sauce	½ tsp.	2 mL
Chopped green onion	½ cup	125 mL
Frozen chopped spinach, thawed and squeezed dry	10 oz.	300 g

Mash first 7 ingredients together with fork in bowl.

Add spinach. Stir. Turn into 3½ quart (3.5 L) slow cooker. Cover. Cook on Low for 1½ hours, stirring every 30 minutes, until quite warm. Makes generous 2 cups (500 mL).

1 tbsp. (15 mL): 29 Calories; 2.2 g Total Fat; 149 mg Sodium; 1 g Protein; 1 g Carbohydrate

Pictured on page 35.

ARTICHOKE DIP

Cream colored. Delicious flavors of Parmesan cheese and artichokes. Serve with chunks of bread.

Light cream cheese, softened	4 oz.	125 g
Salad dressing (or mayonnaise)	½ cup	125 mL
Light sour cream	¼ cup	60 mL
Grated Parmesan cheese	½ cup	125 mL
Garlic powder	¼ tsp.	1 mL
Onion powder	¼ tsp.	1 mL
Chopped green onion	1 tbsp.	15 mL
Jars marinated artichoke hearts, drained and chopped	2 × 6 oz.	2 × 170 mL

Beat cream cheese, salad dressing and sour cream together in bowl until smooth. Stir in Parmesan cheese, garlic powder, onion powder and green onion.

Add artichokes. Turn into 3½ quart (3.5 L) slow cooker. Cook on Low for about 2 hours, stirring occasionally, until quite warm. Makes 2 cups (500 mL).

1 tbsp. (15 mL): 31 Calories; 2.2 g Total Fat; 119 mg Sodium; 1 g Protein; 2 g Carbohydrate

REFRIED BEAN DIP

A smooth bean mixture with cheese and green onion. Serve with chips and vegetables.

Refried beans (less than 1% fat)	14 oz.	398 mL
Grated medium or sharp Cheddar cheese	1 cup	250 mL
Chopped green onion	¼ cup	60 mL
Chili powder	1 tsp.	5 mL

Put beans, cheese, green onion and chili powder into 3½ quart (3.5 L) slow cooker. Stir. Cover. Cook on Low for 1½ hours, stirring every 20 minutes, until melted and quite warm. Makes 2 cups (500 mL).

1 tbsp. (15 mL): 29 Calories; 1.3 g Total Fat; 77 mg Sodium; 2 g Protein; 3 g Carbohydrate

HOT WINGS

Dip these nippy little fellows into Blue Cheese Dip for a special treat.

White vinegar	4 tsp.	20 mL
Granulated sugar	2 tsp.	10 mL
Hot pepper sauce	¼ cup	60 mL
Paprika	1 tsp.	5 mL
Whole chicken wings (or drumettes)	3 lbs.	1.4 kg
BLUE CHEESE DIP		
Light salad dressing (or mayonnaise)	½ cup	125 mL
Blue cheese, crumbled	¼ cup	60 mL
Lemon juice	1 tbsp.	15 mL
Onion powder	¼ tsp.	1 mL
Garlic powder	¼ tsp.	1 mL
Worcestershire sauce	½ tsp.	2 mL
Non-fat (or regular) sour cream	½ cup	125 mL

Combine first 4 ingredients in small cup. Stir. Discard tip and cut wings apart at joint. Brush sauce over both sides of chicken pieces. Place pieces in 3½ quart (3.5 L) slow cooker. Cover. Cook on Low for 7 to 8 hours or on High for 3½ to 4 hours until tender. Serve from slow cooker. Makes about 28 pieces of wing or 18 drumettes.

Blue Cheese Dip: Combine all 7 ingredients in bowl. Beat until smooth. Makes 1⅛ cups (280 mL). Serve with wings.

1 wing piece (with dip): 81 Calories; 5.8 g Total Fat; 76 mg Sodium; 5 g Protein; 1 g Carbohydrate

1. Cranberry Warmer, page 57
2. Sweet And Sour Wings, page 12
3. Curried Almonds, page 11
4. Carrot Onion Casserole, page 150
5. Stuffed Pork Roast, page 93
6. Applesauce, page 79
7. Snack Mix, page 10

Props Courtesy Of: Eaton's; Stokes;
The Basket House;
The Bay

CHILI CON QUESO

South of the border. Great served with chips.

Velveeta cheese, cubed	**1 lb.**	**454 g**
Canned chopped green chilies	**4 oz.**	**114 mL**
Medium or hot salsa	**1¼ cups**	**300 mL**

Combine cheese, green chilies and salsa in 3½ quart (3.5 L) slow cooker. Stir. Cover. Cook on Low for 1½ hours, stirring occasionally, until quite warm. Makes a generous 3 cups (750 mL).

1 tbsp. (15 mL): 34 Calories; 2.2 g Total Fat; 258 mg Sodium; 2 g Protein; 2 g Carbohydrate

ORIENTAL CHICKEN WINGS

Soy sauce flavor is always a favorite. These marinate as they cook.

Whole chicken wings (or drumettes)	**3 lbs.**	**1.4 kg**
Soy sauce	**1 cup**	**250 mL**
Brown sugar, packed	**¾ cup**	**175 mL**
Water	**½ cup**	**125 mL**
Lemon juice	**1 tsp.**	**5 mL**
Dry mustard	**¼ tsp.**	**1 mL**
Garlic powder	**¼ tsp.**	**1 mL**
Salt	**½ tsp.**	**2 mL**
Ground ginger	**¼ tsp.**	**1 mL**

Discard tip and cut wings apart at joint. Place pieces in 3½ quart (3.5 L) slow cooker.

Measure remaining 8 ingredients into bowl. Mix well. Pour over chicken pieces. Cover. Cook on Low for 8 to 9 hours or on High for 4 to 4½ hours until tender. Serve from slow cooker or remove to platter. Makes about 28 pieces of wing or about 18 drumettes.

1 wing piece (with sauce): 91 Calories; 4.3 g Total Fat; 692 mg Sodium; 6 g Protein; 7 g Carbohydrate

Paré Pointer

If you have a rabbit and a lawn sprinkler, you have hare spray.

BEEF 'N' BEANS

Lots of beef, beans and rice. A meal in one.

Lean ground beef	1 lb.	454 g
Canned mixed beans, with liquid	19 oz.	540 mL
Canned black-eyed peas, with liquid	14 oz.	398 mL
Canned tomatoes, with juice, broken up	14 oz.	398 mL
Finely chopped onion	1/2 cup	125 mL
Mild or medium salsa	1 cup	250 mL
Uncooked long grain converted rice	2/3 cup	150 mL
Salt	1 tsp.	5 mL
Pepper	1/4 tsp.	1 mL
Garlic powder	1/4 tsp.	1 mL
Water	1 cup	250 mL

Scramble-fry ground beef in non-stick frying pan. Drain well. Turn into 3¹/₂ quart (3.5 L) slow cooker.

Add remaining 10 ingredients. Stir. Cover. Cook on Low for 8 to 9 hours or on High for 4 to 4¹/₂ hours. Makes a generous 8 cups (2 L).

1 cup (250 mL): 281 Calories; 5.7 g Total Fat; 1303 mg Sodium; 19 g Protein; 39 g Carbohydrate; excellent source of Dietary Fiber

OVERNIGHT BAKED BEANS

When you start the beans cooking, have the rest of the ingredients measured and ready to add when needed.

Dried navy beans	2 cups	500 mL
Water	4 cups	1 L
Diced bacon, cooked crisp (about 5 slices)	3/4 cup	175 mL
Ketchup	1/4 cup	60 mL
Brown sugar, packed	1/3 cup	75 mL
Molasses (not blackstrap)	2 tbsp.	30 mL

Combine beans and water in 3¹/₂ quart (3.5 L) slow cooker. Stir well. Cover. Cook on Low for 8 to 10 hours or overnight until beans are soft.

Add remaining 4 ingredients. Stir well. Cover. Cook on High for about 30 minutes to blend flavors. Makes 4 cups (1 L).

¹/₂ cup (125 mL): 256 Calories; 2.7 g Total Fat; 183 mg Sodium; 13 g Protein; 47 g Carbohydrate; good source of Dietary Fiber

Saucy, beany and meaty. Serve with crusty rolls.

Dried chick peas (garbanzo beans), 2½ cups (625 mL)	1 lb.	454 g
Chopped onion	1½ cups	375 mL
Medium carrots, cut julienne	2	2
Dried sweet basil	½ tsp.	2 mL
Pepper	¼ tsp.	1 mL
Water	5½ cups	1.4 L
Beef (or pork) stew meat, cut into ½ inch (12 mm) cubes	1 lb.	454 g
Cooking oil	1½ tsp.	7 mL
Canned tomatoes, drained, juice reserved	14 oz.	398 mL
Beef bouillon powder	1 tbsp.	15 mL
Salt	1 tsp.	5 mL
Reserved tomato juice		
All-purpose flour	3 tbsp.	50 mL

Combine first 6 ingredients in 3½ quart (3.5 L) slow cooker.

Brown beef quickly in hot cooking oil in frying pan. Add to slow cooker. Cover. Cook on Low for 8 to 10 hours or on High for 4 to 5 hours.

Add tomato, bouillon powder and salt.

Slowly whisk tomato juice into flour in small bowl. Stir into slow cooker. Cover. Cook on Low for 2 hours or on High for 1 hour. Stir before serving. Makes 9½ cups (2.3 L).

1 cup (250 mL): 300 Calories; 8.1 g Total Fat; 589 mg Sodium; 21 g Protein; 37 g Carbohydrate

Pictured on page 125.

Paré Pointer

If you hear a loud knock, it isn't opportunity. It's a relative.

BOSTON BAKED BEANS

When served as a breakfast dish in Boston in years past, it contained diced salt pork.

Dried navy beans (or peas), 1 lb. (454 g)	2¼ cups	560 mL
Chopped onion	1½ cups	375 mL
Water	5 cups	1.25 L
Ketchup	½ cup	125 mL
Molasses (not blackstrap)	⅓ cup	75 mL
Brown sugar, packed	⅓ cup	75 mL
Dry mustard	1 tsp.	5 mL
Salt	1 tsp.	5 mL
Pepper	¼ tsp.	1 mL

Combine beans, onion and water in 3½ quart (3.5 L) slow cooker. Stir. Cover. Cook on Low for 8 to 10 hours or on High for 4 to 5 hours.

Add remaining 6 ingredients. Stir well. Cover. Cook on High for about 30 minutes to blend flavors. Makes 6 cups (1.5 L).

½ cup (125 mL): 195 Calories; 0.6 g Total Fat; 380 mg Sodium; 9 g Protein; 40 g Carbohydrate; good source of Dietary Fiber

RANCH-STYLE BEANS

Thick and meaty. A touch on the sweet side. Contains both beef and ham.

Extra lean ground beef	1 lb.	454 g
Diced smoked ham (or 1 can, 6.5 oz., 184 g, with liquid)	1 cup	250 mL
Chopped onion	1 cup	250 mL
Canned beans in tomato sauce	2 x 14 oz.	2 x 398 mL
Canned kidney beans, drained	19 oz.	540 mL
Ketchup	½ cup	125 mL
Molasses (not blackstrap)	¼ cup	60 mL
Brown sugar, packed	¼ cup	60 mL
Salt	¾ tsp.	4 mL
Pepper	⅛ tsp.	0.5 mL
Liquid gravy browner	¼ tsp.	1 mL

Measure all 11 ingredients into 3½ quart (3.5 L) slow cooker. Mix well to break up and distribute beef and ham. Cover. Cook on Low for 8 to 9 hours or on High for 4 to 4½ hours. Stir before serving. Makes 8 cups (2 L).

1 cup (250 mL): 385 Calories; 9.7 g Total Fat; 1273 mg Sodium; 27 g Protein; 51 g Carbohydrate; excellent source of Dietary Fiber

A variety of pastel colors—green, yellow and cream—with little bits of red showing. A hearty vegetable.

Frozen lima beans	2 cups	500 mL
Chopped onion	1½ cups	375 mL
Sliced celery	½ cup	125 mL
Frozen corn	2 cups	500 mL
Chopped pimiento	2 tbsp.	30 mL
Garlic powder	¼ tsp.	1 mL
Dried sweet basil	¼ tsp.	1 mL
Salt	½ tsp.	2 mL
Pepper	⅛ tsp.	0.5 mL
Condensed cream of mushroom soup	10 oz.	284 mL

Grated medium Cheddar cheese, sprinkle

Measure first 10 ingredients into large bowl. Stir together well. Put into 3½ quart (3.5 L) slow cooker. Cover. Cook on Low for 8 to 10 hours or on High for 4 to 5 hours.

Stir. Sprinkle with cheese before serving. Makes 4 cups (1 L).

½ cup (125 mL): 136 Calories; 3.4 g Total Fat; 509 mg Sodium; 5 g Protein; 24 g Carbohydrate; good source of Dietary Fiber

Pictured on page 107.

Paré Pointer

If you meet a fire-breathing dragon, douse him with water so he'll let off steam.

BEANS AND BACON

To have more of a nip, use medium salsa. A touch on the sweet side. Good mixture.

Bacon slices, diced	8	8
Canned beans in tomato sauce, drained	2 × 14 oz.	2 × 398 mL
Chopped onion	1 cup	250 mL
Medium green pepper, chopped	1	1
Brown sugar, packed	½ cup	125 mL
Ketchup	½ cup	125 mL
Worcestershire sauce	1 tsp.	5 mL
Liquid smoke	¼-½ tsp.	1-2 mL
Mild or medium salsa	½ cup	125 mL
Prepared mustard	1 tsp.	5 mL

Cook bacon in frying pan until crispy. Drain well. Turn into 3½ quart (3.5 L) slow cooker.

Add remaining 9 ingredients. Stir. Cover. Cook on Low for 6 to 7 hours or on High for 3 to 3½ hours. Makes 6 cups (1.5 L).

½ cup (125 mL): 153 Calories; 2.5 g Total Fat; 670 mg Sodium; 5 g Protein; 30 g Carbohydrate; excellent source of Dietary Fiber

PINEAPPLE BAKED BEANS

The pineapple flavor really complements this dish.

Canned beans in tomato sauce, with liquid	2 × 14 oz.	2 × 398 mL
Canned kidney beans, drained	14 oz.	398 mL
Minced onion flakes	3 tbsp.	50 mL
Hickory smoked barbecue sauce	½ cup	125 mL
Canned crushed pineapple, drained	14 oz.	398 mL
Brown sugar, packed	½ cup	125 mL
Prepared mustard	1½ tsp.	7 mL

Place all 7 ingredients in 3½ quart (3.5 L) slow cooker. Stir well. Cover. Cook on Low for 6 to 8 hours or on High for 3 to 4 hours. Makes 6½ cups (1.6 L).

½ cup (125 mL): 140 Calories; 0.6 g Total Fat; 397 mg Sodium; 5 g Protein; 31 g Carbohydrate; excellent source of Dietary Fiber

Tastes just like lasagne but doesn't have layers.

Lasagne noodles, broken into bite-size pieces	8	8
Boiling water	3 qts.	3 L
Cooking oil (optional)	2 tsp.	10 mL
Salt	2 tsp.	10 mL
Lean ground beef	1½ lbs.	680 g
Finely chopped onion	¾ cup	175 mL
Canned tomatoes, with juice, broken up	2 × 14 oz.	2 × 398 mL
Tomato paste	5½ oz.	156 mL
Creamed cottage cheese	1 cup	250 mL
Grated mozzarella cheese	2 cups	500 mL
Granulated sugar	2 tsp.	10 mL
Parsley flakes	1 tsp.	5 mL
Dried whole oregano	½ tsp.	2 mL
Garlic powder	¼ tsp.	1 mL
Dried sweet basil	¼ tsp.	1 mL
Salt	1¼ tsp.	6 mL
Pepper	½ tsp.	2 mL

Cook lasagne noodle pieces in boiling water, cooking oil and salt in large uncovered Dutch oven for 14 to 16 minutes until tender but firm. Drain.

Scramble-fry ground beef in non-stick frying pan until browned. Drain well. Turn into 3½ quart (3.5 L) slow cooker.

Add remaining 12 ingredients. Stir well. Add lasagne noodle pieces. Stir. Cover. Cook on Low for 7 to 9 hours or on High for 3½ to 4½ hours. Makes 10 cups (2.5 L).

1 cup (250 mL): 295 Calories; 12.4 g Total Fat; 708 mg Sodium; 24 g Protein; 22 g Carbohydrate

Paré Pointer

If you smashed a clock, would you be convicted of killing time?

HAMBURGER CASSEROLE

Slight tomato flavor with carrot and peas adding color.

Lean ground beef	1½ lbs.	680 g
Medium potatoes, thinly sliced	3	3
Medium onion, thinly sliced	1	1
Medium carrots, thinly sliced	3	3
Celery rib, thinly sliced	1	1
Frozen peas	10 oz.	300 g
Salt	1 tsp.	5 mL
Pepper	¼ tsp.	1 mL
Condensed tomato soup	10 oz.	284 mL
Beef bouillon powder	2 tsp.	10 mL
Water	½ cup	125 mL

Scramble-fry ground beef in frying pan until browned. Drain well. Turn into 3½ quart (3.5 L) slow cooker.

Add next 7 ingredients. Stir.

Mix soup, bouillon powder and water in bowl. Add to slow cooker. Stir. Cover. Cook on Low for 8 to 10 hours or on High for 4 to 5 hours. Makes 8 cups (2 L).

1 cup (250 mL): 238 Calories; 8 g Total Fat; 842 mg Sodium; 19 g Protein; 22 g Carbohydrate; good source of Dietary Fiber

HAMBURGER STROGANOFF

Stroganoff over noodles makes a favorite dish.

Lean ground beef	1½ lbs.	680 g
All-purpose flour	2 tbsp.	30 mL
Salt	1 tsp.	5 mL
Pepper	¼ tsp.	1 mL
Chopped onion	1 cup	250 mL
Condensed cream of chicken soup	10 oz.	284 mL
Red wine vinegar	1 tsp.	5 mL
Prepared orange juice	2 tbsp.	30 mL
Light sour cream	1 cup	250 mL
Fettuccine noodles	1 lb.	454 g
Boiling water	4 qts.	4 L
Cooking oil (optional)	1 tbsp.	15 mL
Salt	1 tbsp.	15 mL

(continued on next page)

Scramble-fry ground beef in non-stick frying pan until browned. Do not drain.

Mix in flour, first amount of salt, pepper and onion. Stir in soup, vinegar and orange juice. Turn into 3½ quart (3.5 L) slow cooker. Cover. Cook on Low for 5 to 6 hours or on High for 2½ to 3 hours.

Stir in sour cream. Heat through. Makes 5 cups (1.25 L).

Cook noodles in boiling water, cooking oil and second amount of salt in large uncovered Dutch oven for 5 to 7 minutes until tender. Drain. Serve stroganoff over noodles. Serves 6.

1 serving: 631 Calories; 24.1 g Total Fat; 946 mg Sodium; 34 g Protein; 67 g Carbohydrate

BEEF STROGANOFF

Rich tasting and colorful. Does double duty. Serve as-is or as a topping for noodles or rice.

All-purpose flour	⅓ cup	75 mL
Salt	1 tsp.	5 mL
Pepper	¼ tsp.	1 mL
Paprika	½ tsp.	2 mL
Beef round steak, cut into ½ inch (12 mm) thick strips	2 lbs.	900 g
Chopped onion	1½ cups	375 mL
Garlic powder	¼ tsp.	1 mL
Canned tomatoes, with juice, broken up	14 oz.	398 mL
Ketchup	¼ cup	60 mL
Beef bouillon powder	2 tsp.	10 mL
Sherry (or alcohol-free sherry)	2 tbsp.	30 mL
Sliced fresh mushrooms	2 cups	500 mL
Light sour cream	1 cup	250 mL

Combine flour, salt, pepper and paprika in plastic bag. Place a few strips of steak in at a time. Shake to coat. Place in 3½ quart (3.5 L) slow cooker.

Mix next 7 ingredients in bowl. Pour over steak. Cover. Cook on Low for 7 to 9 hours or on High for 3½ to 4½ hours.

Stir in sour cream last 30 minutes of cooking time. Serves 6.

1 serving: 365 Calories; 13.6 g Total Fat; 1008 mg Sodium; 40 g Protein; 19 g Carbohydrate

SPICY SPAGHETTI SAUCE

Serve this over spaghetti, noodles or other pasta. A chunky sauce.

Canned diced tomatoes	19 oz.	540 mL
Ketchup	1/4 cup	60 mL
Canned sliced mushrooms, drained	10 oz.	284 mL
Chopped green pepper	1/3 cup	75 mL
Lemon juice	1 1/2 tbsp.	25 mL
Dried whole oregano	3/4 tsp.	4 mL
Dried sweet basil	1/2 tsp.	2 mL
Bay leaf	1	1
Chili powder	2 tsp.	10 mL
Garlic powder	1/4 tsp.	1 mL
Granulated sugar (optional)	1 tsp.	5 mL
Salt	1 1/2 tsp.	7 mL
Pepper	1/4 tsp.	1 mL
Lean ground beef	1 lb.	454 g
Chopped onion	1 cup	250 mL

Combine first 13 ingredients in 3 1/2 quart (3.5 L) slow cooker.

Scramble-fry ground beef and onion in non-stick frying pan until beef is no longer pink. Drain well. Add to slow cooker. Stir. Cover. Cook on Low for 6 to 7 hours or on High for 3 to 3 1/2 hours. Discard bay leaf. Makes 5 1/4 cups (1.3 L).

1 cup (250 mL): 193 Calories; 7.8 g Total Fat; 1267 mg Sodium; 18 g Protein; 14 g Carbohydrate; good source of Dietary Fiber

Pictured on page 107.

BEEFY RICE CASSEROLE

A mild chili flavor addition. Good mixture.

Cooking oil	1 tbsp.	15 mL
Lean ground beef	1 1/2 lbs.	680 g
Canned tomatoes, with juice	28 oz.	796 mL
Chopped onion	1 1/2 cups	375 mL
Chopped green pepper	1/4 cup	60 mL
Uncooked long grain converted rice	1 cup	250 mL
Salt	1 1/2 tsp.	7 mL
Chili powder	1 tsp.	5 mL
Water	1 cup	250 mL

(continued on next page)

Heat cooking oil in frying pan. Add ground beef. Scramble-fry until browned. Drain well. Turn into 3½ quart (3.5 L) slow cooker.

Add remaining 7 ingredients. Stir. Cover. Cook on Low for 6 to 8 hours or on High for 3 to 4 hours. Makes 7½ cups (1.8 L).

1 cup (250 mL): 285 Calories; 7.4 g Total Fat; 766 mg Sodium; 14 g Protein; 29 g Carbohydrate

MEATY SPAGHETTI SAUCE

Thick dark reddish sauce with just the right spice mixture. Leftover sauce may be frozen.

Canned tomatoes, with juice, mashed	28 oz.	796 mL
Tomato paste	5½ oz.	156 mL
Finely chopped onion	1 cup	250 mL
Garlic powder	½ tsp.	2 mL
Prepared mustard	2 tsp.	10 mL
Dried whole oregano	½ tsp.	2 mL
Parsley flakes	1 tsp.	5 mL
Granulated sugar	2 tsp.	10 mL
Bay leaf	1	1
Liquid gravy browner	½ tsp.	2 mL
Beef bouillon powder	1 tsp.	5 mL
Salt	1¼ tsp.	6 mL
Pepper	¼ tsp.	1 mL
Lean ground beef	1 lb.	454 g
Canned sliced mushrooms, drained	10 oz.	284 mL

Combine first 13 ingredients in large bowl. Stir well.

Add ground beef and mushrooms. Mix. Turn into 3½ quart (3.5 L) slow cooker. Cover. Cook on Low for 7 to 9 hours or on High for 3½ to 4½ hours. Discard bay leaf. Makes 6 cups (1.5 L).

½ cup (125 mL): 121 Calories; 6.1 g Total Fat; 546 mg Sodium; 9 g Protein; 8 g Carbohydrate

CHILI

Nice mild and dark chili. To make more fiery, simply add more chili powder.

Lean ground beef	1 lb.	454 g
Chopped onion	1 cup	250 mL
Green pepper, chopped	1	1
Canned kidney beans, with liquid	14 oz.	398 mL
Canned sliced mushrooms, drained	10 oz.	284 mL
Condensed tomato soup	10 oz.	284 mL
Chili powder	1 tsp.	5 mL
Seasoning salt	1/4 tsp.	1 mL
Granulated sugar	1 tsp.	5 mL
Salt	1/2 tsp.	2 mL
Pepper	1/8 tsp.	0.5 mL

Scramble-fry ground beef in non-stick frying pan until browned. Drain well.

Place onion and green pepper in bottom of 3 1/2 quart (3.5 L) slow cooker.

Combine remaining 8 ingredients in bowl. Stir well. Add ground beef. Stir. Add to slow cooker. Cover. Cook on Low for 6 to 7 hours or on High for 3 to 3 1/2 hours. Stir before serving. Makes 5 1/2 cups (1.3 L).

1 cup (250 mL): 252 Calories; 8.2 g Total Fat; 1109 mg Sodium; 21 g Protein; 25 g Carbohydrate; excellent source of Dietary Fiber

PANIC ROAST!

Take roast out of freezer and place in slow cooker without defrosting. Make this easy one-step roast when time is of the essence.

Frozen boneless beef roast	3 lbs.	1.4 kg
Boiling water, to completely cover		

Place roast in 3 1/2 quart (3.5 L) slow cooker. Pour boiling water over top. Cover. Cook on Low for 7 to 8 hours. Serves 10.

1 serving: 230 Calories; 9.5 g Total Fat; 78 mg Sodium; 34 g Protein; 0 g Carbohydrate

SWISS STEAK MEDITERRANEAN

Lots of deep rusty red gravy with steak, onion and mushrooms.

Spaghetti sauce	2 cups	500 mL
Dried whole oregano	1/2 tsp.	2 mL
Salt	1 tsp.	5 mL
Pepper	1/4 tsp.	1 mL
Beef round steak, trimmed of fat, cut into 6 pieces	1³/₄ lbs.	790 g
Medium onions, cut into chunks	2	2
Small whole fresh mushrooms (about 2 cups, 500 mL)	1/2 lb.	225 g

Stir first 4 ingredients together in bowl.

Place steak pieces in 3¹/₂ quart (3.5 L) slow cooker. Pour ¹/₃ of sauce over and between pieces.

Sprinkle onion and mushrooms over top. Pour remaining ²/₃ of sauce over all. Cover. Cook on Low for 7 to 9 hours or on High for 3¹/₂ to 4¹/₂ hours. Serves 6.

1 serving: 253 Calories; 7.4 g Total Fat; 943 mg Sodium; 28 g Protein, 19 g Carbohydrate

Pictured on page 35.

AEGEAN BEEF

Spiced with oregano and thyme.

Boneless beef chuck steak, cut into 1¹/₂ inch (3.8 cm) cubes	2.2 lbs.	1 kg
Chopped or sliced onion	2 cups	500 mL
Condensed cream of chicken soup	10 oz.	284 mL
Dried whole oregano	1/2 tsp.	2 mL
Ground thyme	1/4 tsp.	1 mL
Salt	³/₄ tsp.	4 mL
Pepper	1/4 tsp.	1 mL
Liquid gravy browner	1/2 tsp.	2 mL

Place beef cubes in 3¹/₂ quart (3.5 L) slow cooker. Add onion over top.

Mix remaining 6 ingredients in bowl. Pour over top. Cover. Cook on Low for 7 to 9 hours or on High for 3¹/₂ to 4¹/₂ hours. Serves 8.

1 serving: 337 Calories; 23.7 g Total Fat; 645 mg Sodium; 23 g Protein; 7 g Carbohydrate

BEEF BRISKET

Brown and tender with chunks of carrot as well. Use leftover meat for sandwiches.

Medium carrots, cut diagonally into thin slices	6	6
Boneless beef brisket, trimmed of fat	4½ lbs.	2 kg
Red (or alcohol-free) wine	½ cup	125 mL
Water	½ cup	125 mL
Beef bouillon powder	2 tsp.	10 mL
Onion powder	½ tsp.	2 mL
Liquid gravy browner	½ tsp.	2 mL
Ground rosemary	¼ tsp.	1 mL
Pepper	¼ tsp.	1 mL

Place carrot in 6 quart (6 L) slow cooker. Lay brisket over top. If cooker is smaller, cut brisket in half.

Combine 7 remaining ingredients in small bowl. Pour over top. Cover. Cook on Low for 10 to 12 hours or on High for 5 to 6 hours until very tender. Serves 12.

1 serving: 243 Calories; 10.1 g Total Fat; 190 mg Sodium; 30 g Protein; 5 g Carbohydrate

POT ROAST

An old-fashioned meal in a pot.

Medium potatoes, cut into chunks	4	4
Medium carrots, cut into chunks (or use peeled baby carrots)	4	4
Medium onions, cut into chunks	2	2
Boneless beef chuck roast (or other)	3 lbs.	1.4 kg
Boiling water	½ cup	125 mL
Beef bouillon powder	1 tsp.	5 mL
Liquid gravy browner	½ tsp.	2 mL

Lay potato, carrot and onion in bottom of 5 quart (5 L) slow cooker.

Place roast on top.

Combine remaining 3 ingredients in small bowl. Stir. Pour over top. Cover. Cook on Low for 10 to 12 hours or on High for 5 to 6 hours. Serves 8 to 10.

⅛ recipe: 302 Calories; 9.9 g Total Fat; 182 mg Sodium; 35 g Protein; 17 g Carbohydrate

Pictured on front cover.

CHILI CON CARNE

A great chili with lots of beans and beef.

Canned tomatoes, with juice, broken up	14 oz.	398 mL
Envelope dry onion soup mix	1 × 1½ oz.	1 × 42 g
Pepper	¼ tsp.	1 mL
Chili powder	2 tsp.	10 mL
Ketchup	¼ cup	60 mL
Liquid gravy browner	½ tsp.	2 mL
Garlic powder (optional)	¼ tsp.	1 mL
Dried sweet basil	¼ tsp.	1 mL
Chopped onion	2 cups	500 mL
Canned kidney beans, with liquid	2 × 14 oz.	2 × 398 mL
Lean ground beef	1½ lbs.	680 g

Combine first 10 ingredients in 3½ quart (3.5 L) or 5 quart (5 L) slow cooker. Stir well.

Scramble-fry ground beef in non-stick frying pan until browned. Drain. Add to slow cooker. Stir. Cover. Cook on Low for 8 to 9 hours or on High for 4 to 4½ hours. Makes 8 cups (2 L).

1 cup (250 mL): 270 Calories; 8 g Total Fat; 1085 mg Sodium; 23 g Protein; 28 g Carbohydrate; excellent source of Dietary Fiber

STUFFED STEAK

Stuffing changes this steak into a scrumptious completely different dish. Also called Mock Duck.

Beef round steak, trimmed of fat, pounded ¼ inch (6 mm) thick	1¾ lbs.	790 g
Box of stuffing mix, prepared as per package directions	4¼ oz.	120 g
Beef bouillon powder	2 tsp.	10 mL
Hot water	1½ cups	375 mL

Lay steak out on flat surface. Spread stuffing over top. Roll up. Tie with string. Depending on size of your slow cooker, you may need to cut beef roll into 2 pieces, such as for the 3½ quart (3.5 L) slow cooker.

Stir bouillon powder into hot water. Pour over all. Cover. Cook on Low for 8 to 10 hours or on High for 4 to 5 hours. Cuts into 10 slices.

1 slice: 146 Calories; 4.6 g Total Fat; 337 mg Sodium; 17 g Protein; 9 g Carbohydrate

HUNGARIAN GOULASH

Super good dish. Beef cubes cook in a medium-thick gravy.

Beef stew meat (or round steak), cut into ¾ inch (2 cm) cubes	1½ lbs.	680 g
Chopped onion	1½ cups	375 mL
Garlic clove, minced (or ¼ tsp., 1 mL, garlic powder)	1	1
All-purpose flour	2 tbsp.	30 mL
Paprika	2 tsp.	10 mL
Salt	1 tsp.	5 mL
Pepper	¼ tsp.	1 mL
Canned tomatoes, with liquid	14 oz.	398 mL
Liquid gravy browner	½ tsp.	2 mL
Beef bouillon powder	2 tsp.	10 mL
Granulated sugar	1 tsp.	5 mL
Sour cream	½-1 cup	125-250 mL

Combine first 7 ingredients in 3½ quart (3.5 L) slow cooker. Stir well to coat beef and onion with flour.

Stir tomato, gravy browner, bouillon powder and sugar together in bowl. Pour over beef mixture. Stir. Cover. Cook on Low for 8 to 10 hours or on High for 4 to 5 hours.

Spoon off a few spoonfuls of juice into bowl. Add sour cream. Stir. Pour back into slow cooker. Stir before serving. Serves 6.

1 serving: 272 Calories; 13.1 g Total Fat; 851 mg Sodium; 27 g Protein; 11 g Carbohydrate

1. Swiss Steak Mediterranean, page 31
2. Scalloped Potatoes, page 110
3. Salmon Loaf, page 86
4. Tasty Mex Casserole, page 49
5. Spinach Dip, page 14

Props Courtesy Of: La Cache; Le Gnome; Stokes; The Bay; Tile Town Ltd.

Dark meatloaf with kidney beans peeping through. Enchilada sauce adds the final touch.

ENCHILADA SAUCE		
Condensed cream of mushroom soup	10 oz.	284 mL
Canned tomatoes, with juice, broken up	14 oz.	398 mL
Canned chopped green chilies	4 oz.	114 mL
Sour cream	¼ cup	60 mL
Granulated sugar	1 tsp.	5 mL
Garlic powder	⅛ tsp.	0.5 mL
Onion powder	⅛ tsp.	0.5 mL

MEATLOAF		
Large eggs, fork-beaten	2	2
Canned tomatoes, with juice, broken up	14 oz.	398 mL
Canned kidney beans, drained	14 oz.	398 mL
Minced onion	½ cup	125 mL
Chili powder	1 tbsp.	15 mL
Salt	2 tsp.	10 mL
Pepper	¼ tsp.	1 mL
Dried whole oregano, generous measure	½ tsp.	2 mL
Garlic powder	¼ tsp.	1 mL
White vinegar	1½ tbsp.	25 mL
Lean ground beef	2 lbs.	900 g
Coarsely crushed corn chips	¾ cup	175 mL
Grated medium or sharp Cheddar cheese	¾ cup	175 mL

Enchilada Sauce: Combine all 7 ingredients in bowl. Stir well. Set aside.

Meatloaf: Combine first 10 ingredients in large bowl. Measure ¼ cup (60 mL) enchilada sauce and add to tomato mixture. Mix well. Cover remaining sauce and refrigerate until meatloaf is done.

Add ground beef and corn chips. Mix very well. Shape into round loaf. Pack in 5 quart (5 L) slow cooker. Cover. Cook on Low for 8 to 10 hours or on High for 4 to 5 hours.

Transfer remaining enchilada sauce to saucepan. Heat, stirring often, until hot. Pour over meatloaf. Sprinkle with cheese. Cook on High until cheese is just melted. Serves 10.

1 serving: 357 Calories; 22.5 g Total Fat; 1189 mg Sodium; 24 g Protein; 15 g Carbohydrate

MEATLOAF STEW

Quite different to have meatloaf in a stew.

Water	¼ cup	60 mL
Medium potatoes, peeled and cut bite size	5-6	5-6
Medium carrots, peeled and cut bite size	6	6
Salt, sprinkle		
Pepper, sprinkle		
Large egg, fork-beaten	1	1
Ketchup	⅓ cup	75 mL
Beef bouillon powder	2 tsp.	10 mL
Finely chopped onion	⅓ cup	75 mL
Ground thyme	¼ tsp.	1 mL
Water	¼ cup	60 mL
Soda cracker crumbs	⅓ cup	75 mL
Salt	1 tsp.	5 mL
Pepper	¼ tsp.	1 mL
Lean ground beef	1½ lbs.	680 g

Pour first amount of water into 6 quart (6 L) slow cooker. Add potato and carrot. Sprinkle with first amounts of salt and pepper.

Combine next 9 ingredients in bowl. Mix well.

Add ground beef. Mix well. Place over vegetables. Cover. Cook on Low for 8 to 10 hours or on High for 4 to 5 hours. Serves 6.

1 serving: 409 Calories; 18.9 g Total Fat; 1010 mg Sodium; 26 g Protein; 34 g Carbohydrate; good source of Dietary Fiber

EASY MEATLOAF

An extra good meatloaf.

Large eggs, fork-beaten	2	2
Ketchup	6 tbsp.	100 mL
Envelope dry onion soup mix	1 × 1½ oz.	1 × 42 g
Quick-cooking rolled oats (not instant)	½ cup	125 mL
Garlic powder	⅛ tsp.	0.5 mL
Parsley flakes	1 tsp.	5 mL
Salt	½ tsp.	2 mL
Lean ground beef	2 lbs.	900 g
Ketchup	3 tbsp.	50 mL

(continued on next page)

Combine first 7 ingredients in large bowl.

Add ground beef. Mix well. Place in 3½ quart (3.5 L) slow cooker.

Smooth second amount of ketchup over top. Cover. Cook on Low for 6 to 8 hours or on High for 3 to 4 hours. Serves 8.

1 serving: 318 Calories; 18.9 g Total Fat; 961 mg Sodium; 24 g Protein; 12 g Carbohydrate

TRADITIONAL MEATLOAF

Cheese adds extra protein and more flavor. Good spices added.

Large eggs, fork-beaten	2	2
Milk	¼ cup	60 mL
Dry bread crumbs	1 cup	250 mL
Worcestershire sauce	1 tsp.	5 mL
Salt	1 tsp.	5 mL
Pepper	¼ tsp.	1 mL
Dried sweet basil	¼ tsp.	1 mL
Ground thyme	¼ tsp.	1 mL
Finely chopped onion	2 cups	500 mL
Lean ground beef	1 lb.	454 g
Lean ground pork	1 lb.	454 g
Grated sharp Cheddar cheese (optional)	1 cup	250 mL
Ketchup	¼ cup	60 mL

Mix first 9 ingredients in large bowl.

Add ground beef and ground pork. Mix well. Press ½ of meat mixture into bottom of greased 5 quart (5 L) slow cooker.

Spread with cheese. Press second ½ of meat mixture over top. Cover. Cook on Low for 10 to 11 hours or on High for 5 to 5½ hours. Smooth ketchup over meat mixture during last hour of cooking. Serves 6 to 8.

⅙ recipe: 405 Calories; 18 g Total Fat; 875 mg Sodium; 36 g Protein; 23 g Carbohydrate

Paré Pointer

If you don't get everything you want, think of the things you do get that you don't want.

BEEF DIP

Lean over bowls of dipping sauce, dunk and enjoy.

Boneless beef chuck (or blade) roast	2½ lbs.	1.1 kg
Boiling water		
Beef bouillon powder	4 tsp.	20 mL
Onion powder	½ tsp.	2 mL
Salt	½ tsp.	2 mL
Pepper	⅛ tsp.	0.5 mL
Hamburger buns, split (buttered, optional)	10	10

Place roast in 3½ quart (3.5 L) slow cooker. Add boiling water until halfway up sides of roast. Cover. Cook on Low for 7 to 9 hours or on High for 3½ to 4½ hours. Remove roast. Strain beef juice. Skim off any fat. Add hot water to beef juice, if needed, to make 3 cups (750 mL).

Add bouillon powder, onion powder, salt and pepper. Stir.

Slice beef thinly. Insert slices into each bun. Serve with a small bowl of beef juice for dipping. Makes 10 buns and 3 cups (750 mL) beef juice.

1 bun with ⅓ cup (75 mL) beef juice: 253 Calories; 8.3 g Total Fat; 636 mg Sodium; 19 g Protein; 24 g Carbohydrate

BEEF IN WINE

Just the right amount of wine flavor. Meat is tender with a delicate blend of flavors. Serve over rice or noodles.

Boneless beef blade steak, cut into 2 inch (5 cm) cubes	2⅛ lbs.	1 kg
Hot water	½ cup	125 mL
Beef bouillon powder	2 tsp.	10 mL
Condensed cream of mushroom soup	10 oz.	284 mL
Canned mushroom pieces, drained	10 oz.	284 mL
Envelope onion soup mix	1 × 1½ oz.	1 × 42 g
Red (or alcohol-free) wine	½ cup	125 mL

(continued on next page)

Place beef cubes in 6 quart (6 L) slow cooker.

Stir hot water and bouillon powder together in medium bowl.

Add soup, mushroom pieces, soup mix and wine. Stir. Pour over beef cubes. Cover. Cook on Low for 7 to 9 hours or on High for 3½ to 4½ hours. Makes 6⅔ cups (1.65 L). Serves 6 to 8.

⅙ recipe: 473 Calories; 32.9 g Total Fat; 982 mg Sodium; 31 g Protein; 9 g Carbohydrate

Pictured on page 125.

SWEDISH MEATBALLS

Make a bunch so you can freeze some; cut the recipe in half for a smaller crowd. Gravy adds the extra touch.

Milk	1 cup	250 mL
Fine dry bread crumbs	1¼ cups	300 mL
Large eggs, fork-beaten	2	2
Chopped onion	1¼ cups	300 mL
Salt	1½ tsp.	7 mL
Pepper	¼ tsp.	1 mL
Ground allspice	⅛ tsp.	0.5 mL
Lean ground beef	1½ lbs.	680 g
Lean ground pork	½ lb.	225 g
SAUCE		
All-purpose flour	¼ cup	60 mL
Salt	½ tsp.	2 mL
Condensed beef consommé	10 oz.	284 mL
Water	1 cup	250 mL

Mix first 7 ingredients in bowl. Stir well.

Add ground beef and ground pork. Shape into 1½ inch (3.8 cm) balls. Arrange on broiler tray. Brown quickly under broiler, turning once. Pile balls into 5 quart (5 L) slow cooker.

Sauce: Measure flour and salt in saucepan. Whisk in consommé and water gradually until no lumps remain. Heat until it boils and thickens a bit. Pour over meatballs. Cover. Cook on Low for 8 to 10 hours or on High for 4 to 5 hours. Makes 57 meatballs.

3 meatballs (with sauce): 151 Calories; 7 g Total Fat; 467 mg Sodium; 12 g Protein; 9 g Carbohydrate

PORCUPINE MEATBALLS

Very colorful with rice being the quills.

Lean ground beef	1½ lbs.	680 g
Onion flakes (or ¼ cup, 60 mL, diced onion)	1½ tbsp.	25 mL
Salt	1 tsp.	5 mL
Pepper	¼ tsp.	1 mL
Large egg, fork-beaten	1	1
Uncooked long grain converted rice	⅔ cup	150 mL
Fine dry bread crumbs	½ cup	125 mL
Milk	2 tbsp.	30 mL
Tomato juice	3 cups	750 mL
Water	1 cup	250 mL
Granulated sugar	1 tsp.	5 mL
Salt	½ tsp.	2 mL
Liquid gravy browner	½ tsp.	2 mL

Combine first 8 ingredients in large bowl. Mix well. Shape into 1½ inch (3.8 cm) balls. Place in 3½ quart (3.5 L) slow cooker.

Pour tomato juice and water into bowl. Add sugar, second amount of salt and gravy browner. Stir. Pour over meatballs. Cover. Cook on Low for 8 to 10 hours or on High for 4 to 5 hours. Makes 36 meatballs.

3 meatballs (with sauce): 204 Calories; 9.3 g Total Fat; 652 mg Sodium; 13 g Protein; 16 g Carbohydrate

SMOKY MEATBALLS

A hint of smoked flavor makes these irresistible.

Chili sauce	¾ cup	175 mL
Granulated sugar	⅔ cup	150 mL
Worcestershire sauce	1 tsp.	5 mL
Large egg, fork-beaten	1	1
Water	½ cup	125 mL
Fine dry bread crumbs	⅔ cup	150 mL
Chopped onion	½ cup	125 mL
Liquid smoke	2 tsp.	10 mL
Garlic powder	¼ tsp.	1 mL
Chili powder	1 tsp.	5 mL
Salt	1 tsp.	5 mL
Pepper	¼ tsp.	1 mL
Lean ground beef	1½ lbs.	680 g

(continued on next page)

Measure first 3 ingredients into bowl. Stir well. Set aside.

Combine next 9 ingredients in bowl. Stir well.

Add ground beef. Mix well. Shape into 1½ inch (3.8 cm) balls. Place in 3½ quart (3.5 L) slow cooker. Spoon chili sauce mixture over top, covering all balls that are visible. Cook on Low for 8 to 10 hours or on High for 4 to 5 hours. Makes 36 meatballs.

3 meatballs (with sauce): 221 Calories; 9.4 g Total Fat; 565 mg Sodium; 13 g Protein; 22 g Carbohydrate

PINEAPPLE MEATBALLS

Sure to please with pineapple flavor coming through.

Fine dry bread (or soda cracker) crumbs	¾ cup	175 mL
Milk	2 tbsp.	30 mL
Large eggs, fork-beaten	2	2
Finely chopped onion	¾ cup	175 mL
Garlic powder	¼ tsp.	1 mL
Ground ginger	¼ tsp.	1 mL
Salt	1¼ tsp.	6 mL
Pepper	¼ tsp.	1 mL
Lean ground beef	1½ lbs.	680 g
SAUCE		
Canned crushed pineapple, with juice	14 oz.	398 mL
Brown sugar, packed	1 cup	250 mL
White vinegar	½ cup	125 mL
Soy sauce	3 tbsp.	50 mL
Cornstarch	1 tbsp.	15 mL
Water	1 tbsp.	15 mL

Stir first 8 ingredients together well in bowl.

Add ground beef. Mix well. Shape into 1½ inch (3.8 cm) balls. Place in 3½ quart (3.5 L) or 5 quart (5 L) slow cooker.

Sauce: Put first 4 ingredients into saucepan on medium. Stir. Bring to a boil.

Stir cornstarch and water together in small cup. Stir into boiling mixture until slightly thickened. Pour over meatballs. Cover. Cook on Low for 8 to 10 hours or on High for 4 to 5 hours. Makes about 36 meatballs.

3 meatballs (with sauce): 268 Calories; 9.8 g Total Fat; 653 mg Sodium; 13 g Protein; 32 g Carbohydrate

CURRIED BEEF

Rich dark color with a good tangy taste.

Beef stew meat, cut into 1½ inch (3.8 cm) thick cubes or strips	2 lbs.	900 g
Medium onions, cut into small chunks	2	2
All-purpose flour	3 tbsp.	50 mL
Salt	1½ tsp.	7 mL
Pepper	½ tsp.	2 mL
Garlic powder (or 1 clove, minced)	¼ tsp.	1 mL
Curry powder	1½ tsp.	7 mL
Tomato sauce	2 × 7.5 oz.	2 × 213 mL
Beef bouillon powder	2 tsp.	10 mL
Liquid gravy browner	½ tsp.	2 mL
Granulated sugar	½ tsp.	2 mL

Combine first 7 ingredients in 3½ quart (3.5 L) slow cooker. Stir well to coat with flour.

Stir remaining 4 ingredients in small bowl. Pour over top. Cover. Cook on Low for 8 to 10 hours or on High for 4 to 5 hours. Makes 6 cups (1.5 L).

1 cup (250 mL): 314 Calories; 13.3 g Total Fat; 1425 mg Sodium; 35 g Protein; 13 g Carbohydrate

ORIENTAL BEEF

Pea pods and bean sprouts are added 30 minutes before serving. They add great flavor.

Beef steak, cut across the grain into thin slices	1½ lbs.	680 g
Beef bouillon powder	1 tbsp.	15 mL
Hot water	2 cups	500 mL
Liquid gravy browner	½ tsp.	2 mL
Soy sauce	3 tbsp.	50 mL
Ground ginger	¼ tsp.	1 mL
Garlic powder	¼ tsp.	1 mL
Cornstarch	2 tbsp.	30 mL
Water	2 tbsp.	30 mL
Frozen pea pods, thawed	6 oz.	170 g
Bean sprouts, handful	1	1

(continued on next page)

Place steak strips in 5 quart (5 L) slow cooker.

Stir next 6 ingredients together in bowl. Pour over top. Cover. Cook on Low for 8 to 10 hours or on High for 4 to 5 hours.

Mix cornstarch and second amount of water in small cup. Add to slow cooker. Stir. Stir in pea pods and bean sprouts. Cover. Cook on High for about 20 minutes until thickened and tender. Serves 6 to 8.

1/6 *recipe:* 221 Calories; 8.7 g Total Fat; 907 mg Sodium; 27 g Protein; 7 g Carbohydrate

CORNED BEEF DINNER

Since corned beef is cooked in liquid, vegetables are placed on top which means it takes longer to cook. So good and so colorful.

Boiling water	2 cups	500 mL
Whole cloves	2	2
Brown sugar, packed	1 tbsp.	15 mL
Bay leaf	1	1
Pepper	1/4 tsp.	1 mL
Corned beef	3 1/3 lbs.	1.5 kg
Small cabbage (about 2 lbs., 900 g), cut into 8 wedges	1	1
Medium carrots, cut up	6	6
Medium onions, cut up	2	2
Medium potatoes, peeled and cut up	4	4

Stir first 5 ingredients together in bowl. Pour liquid mixture into 6 quart (6 L) slow cooker.

Place corned beef in liquid mixture.

Add remaining 4 ingredients. Cover. Cook on Low for 10 to 12 hours or on High for 5 to 6 hours. Discard bay leaf. Serves 12.

1 serving: 298 Calories; 17 g Total Fat; 1028 mg Sodium; 18 g Protein; 18 g Carbohydrate; good source of Dietary Fiber

Paré Pointer

If you have a doorbell and a baseball player, you have a dingbat.

BBQ BEEF RIBS

Awesome flavor and so tender.

Cooking oil	2 tbsp.	30 mL
Beef short ribs, trimmed of fat	3 lbs.	1.4 kg
Barbecue sauce	1 cup	250 mL
Molasses (not blackstrap)	2 tbsp.	30 mL
White vinegar	2 tbsp.	30 mL
Salt	1½ tsp.	7 mL
Pepper	½ tsp.	2 mL
Soy sauce	1 tbsp.	15 mL
Chopped onion	½ cup	125 mL

Heat cooking oil in frying pan. Add ribs. Brown all sides. Drain. Place ribs in 5 quart (5 L) slow cooker.

Mix next 6 ingredients well in bowl.

Stir in onion. Pour over short ribs. Cover. Cook on Low for 8 to 10 hours or on High for 4 to 5 hours. Serves 6.

1 serving: 310 Calories; 15.9 g Total Fat; 1415 mg Sodium; 27 g Protein; 13 g Carbohydrate

BEEF SHORT RIBS

A very tender economical meat dish.

Beef short ribs, trimmed of fat	4 lbs.	1.8 kg
Salt, sprinkle		
Pepper, sprinkle		
Medium onions, sliced or chopped	2	2
Beef bouillon powder	2 tsp.	10 mL
Liquid gravy browner	½ tsp.	2 mL
Warm water	1½ cups	375 mL

Sprinkle short ribs with salt and pepper.

Lay onion in bottom of 5 quart (5 L) slow cooker. Arrange ribs over top.

Stir bouillon powder and gravy browner into warm water. Pour over ribs. Cover. Cook on Low for 7 to 9 hours or on High for 3½ to 4½ hours. Serves 8.

1 serving: 215 Calories; 11.9 g Total Fat; 203 mg Sodium; 23 g Protein; 3 g Carbohydrate

POLYNESIAN STEAK STRIPS

This is easy to cut in half for a family of four. Dark strips of beef have a ginger soy sauce flavor.

Beef steak, cut across the grain into thin slices	**2 lbs.**	**900 g**
Water	½ cup	125 mL
Ketchup	2 tbsp.	30 mL
Oyster sauce	1 tbsp.	15 mL
Soy sauce	¼ cup	60 mL
Ground ginger	½ tsp.	2 mL
Garlic powder	¼ tsp.	1 mL
Granulated sugar	1 tsp.	5 mL
Liquid gravy browner	¼ tsp.	1 mL
Salt	1 tsp.	5 mL
Pepper	¼ tsp.	1 mL

Place steak strips in 3½ quart (3.5 L) slow cooker.

Mix remaining 10 ingredients in small bowl. Pour over strips. Stir. Cover. Cook on Low for 8 to 10 hours or on High for 4 to 5 hours. Serves 6.

1 serving: 263 Calories; 11.2 g Total Fat; 1480 mg Sodium; 34 g Protein; 5 g Carbohydrate

Pictured on page 143.

ITALIAN-STYLE ROAST

Topped with red sauce, this is very tender.

Beef sirloin tip roast	**3 lbs.**	**1.4 kg**
Canned mushroom pieces, drained	**10 oz.**	**284 mL**
Chopped onion	**1 cup**	**250 mL**
Spaghetti sauce	**1 cup**	**250 mL**
Garlic salt	**½ tsp.**	**2 mL**

Gravy, page 48

Place roast in 3½ quart (3.5 L) slow cooker. Add mushroom pieces and onion.

Stir spaghetti sauce and garlic salt together in bowl. Pour over all. Cover. Cook on Low for 8 to 10 hours or on High for 4 to 5 hours.

Make gravy with remaining liquid. Serves 6 to 8.

1 serving: 407 Calories; 14.4 g Total Fat; 797 mg Sodium; 54 g Protein; 13 g Carbohydrate

ROAST BEEF

Mmm! Roast beef and gravy. Bring on the potatoes and vegetables.

Boneless beef roast (such as eye of round)	3 lbs.	1.4 kg
Beef bouillon powder	1 tsp.	5 mL
Boiling water	½ cup	125 mL
Gravy, below		

Place beef in 3½ quart (3.5 L) slow cooker.

Stir bouillon powder and boiling water together in small cup. Pour over beef. Cover. Cook on Low for 8 to 10 hours or on High for 4 to 5 hours.

Make gravy with remaining juice from beef. Serves 6 to 8.

1 serving: 396 Calories; 16 g Total Fat; 442 mg Sodium; 57 g Protein; 2 g Carbohydrate

GRAVY

Whether you want a little gravy or a lot, simply use this method.

All-purpose flour	2 tbsp.	30 mL
Salt (see Note)	¼ tsp.	1 mL
Pepper	¹⁄₁₆ tsp.	0.5 mL
Meat juice or liquid, strained if needed, fat removed, plus water to make	1 cup	250 mL
Bouillon powder (use beef bouillon for beef, pork or lamb; chicken bouillon for poultry)	1 tsp.	5 mL
Liquid gravy browner, enough to make a pleasing color (optional)		

Combine flour, salt and pepper in saucepan. Stir.

Gradually whisk in meat juice and water until no lumps remain. Heat and stir until boiling and thickened.

Taste, adding bouillon powder for more flavor if needed. Stir in gravy browner to color. Add more salt and pepper if needed. Makes 1 cup (250 mL).

Note: The more bouillon powder used, the less salt required. Salt may be added as the last step.

¼ cup (60 mL): 17 Calories; 0.1 g Total Fat; 318 mg Sodium; 1 g Protein; 3 g Carbohydrate

Lots of color. Green chilies add flavor.

Lean ground beef	1½ lbs.	680 g
White vinegar	3 tbsp.	50 mL
Chili powder	1 tbsp.	15 mL
Dried whole oregano	1 tsp.	5 mL
Garlic powder	¼ tsp.	1 mL
Salt	1½ tsp.	7 mL
Pepper	¼ tsp.	1 mL
Chopped onion	1½ cups	375 mL
Medium green pepper, chopped	1	1
Canned chopped green chilies drained (optional)	4 oz.	114 mL
Canned kernel corn, drained	12 oz.	341 mL
Elbow macaroni, partially cooked, drained and rinsed	1 cup	250 mL
Canned tomatoes, with juice, broken up	2 × 14 oz.	2 × 398 mL
Chili powder	2 tsp.	10 mL
Parsley flakes	1 tsp.	5 mL
Dried whole oregano	½ tsp.	2 mL
Granulated sugar	2 tsp.	10 mL
Salt	½ tsp.	2 mL
Pepper	¼ tsp.	1 mL

Mix first 7 ingredients in bowl. Scramble-fry in non-stick frying pan until browned. Drain.

Put onion into 3½ quart (3.5 L) or 5 quart (5 L) slow cooker. Add green pepper, green chilies, corn and partially cooked macaroni. Add beef mixture. Stir.

Combine remaining 7 ingredients in bowl. Stir well. Pour over top. Stir. Cover. Cook on Low for 8 hours or on High for 4 hours. Makes 10 cups (2.5 L).

1 cup (250 mL): 206 Calories; 6.5 g Total Fat; 874 mg Sodium; 16 g Protein; 23 g Carbohydrate

Pictured on page 35.

Paré Pointer

If you've been growling all day, you will be dog tired at night.

BEEF BOURGUIGNONNE

Cubes of beef with onion and mushrooms have that food cooked-in-wine taste.

Boneless beef chuck roast, cut into 1 inch (2.5 cm) cubes	1½ lbs.	680 g
Sliced white onion	1 cup	250 mL
Small whole mushrooms	2 cups	500 mL
Condensed cream of mushroom soup	10 oz.	284 mL
Red (or alcohol-free) wine	¼ cup	60 mL
Beef bouillon powder	1 tsp.	5 mL
Water	½ cup	125 mL
Salt	¾ tsp.	4 mL
Pepper	¼ tsp.	1 mL

Place beef cubes in 3½ quart (3.5 L) slow cooker. Add onion and mushrooms.

Combine 6 remaining ingredients in bowl. Stir vigorously. Pour over top. Cover. Cook on Low for 8 to 10 hours or on High for 4 to 5 hours. Serves 6.

1 serving: 193 Calories; 9.7 g Total Fat; 882 mg Sodium; 17 g Protein; 8 g Carbohydrate

STEAK AND MUSHROOMS

In its own gravy. Ready and waiting.

Beef round steak (about 1 inch, 2.5 cm, thick), cut into cubes	1 lb.	454 g
Salt, sprinkle		
Pepper, sprinkle		
Condensed cream of mushroom soup	10 oz.	284 mL
Canned mushroom pieces, drained (optional)	10 oz.	284 mL
Liquid gravy browner	¼ tsp.	1 mL

Place beef cubes in 3½ quart (3.5 L) slow cooker. Sprinkle with salt and pepper.

Combine soup and mushroom pieces in bowl. Add gravy browner. Stir well. Spoon over steak. Cover. Cook on Low for 7 to 9 hours or on High for 3½ to 4½ hours. Serves 4.

1 serving: 265 Calories; 13.4 g Total Fat; 685 mg Sodium; 29 g Protein: 6 g Carbohydrate

HOT CITRUS PUNCH

A pretty bright yellow. Nice light tang. Good sipping.

Prepared orange juice	4 cups	1 L
Frozen concentrated lemonade, thawed	12½ oz.	355 mL
Lemon-lime soft drink	4 cups	1 L
Ginger ale	4 cups	1 L

Combine all 4 ingredients in 3½ quart (3.5 L) slow cooker. Stir. Cover. Cook on Low for at least 3 hours until quite warm. Makes 12⅔ cups (3.1 L)

1 cup (250 mL): 159 Calories; 0.1 g Total Fat; 17 mg Sodium; 1 g Protein; 41 g Carbohydrate

Pictured on front cover.

APPLE PUNCH

Cinnamon-apple flavor. A great cold day sipper. Doubles or triples easily.

Apple juice	4⅓ cups	1 L
Brown sugar, packed	1 tbsp.	15 mL
Lemon juice	½ tsp.	2 mL
Cinnamon stick (2 inches, 5 cm, in length), broken up and crushed in plastic bag	1	1
Whole cloves	15	15
Orange pekoe tea bag (or 1 tbsp., 15 mL, loose tea)	1	1

Combine apple juice, brown sugar and lemon juice in 3½ quart (3.5 L) slow cooker. Stir.

Tie cinnamon, cloves and tea bag in double layer of cheesecloth. Add to slow cooker. Cover. Heat on Low for at least 3 hours until quite warm. Discard spice bag. Makes 4 cups (1 L).

1 cup (250 mL): 150 Calories; 0.3 g Total Fat; 17 mg Sodium; trace Protein; 38 g Carbohydrate

Pictured on page 125.

MULLED WINE

A very convenient potful, ready for company.

Dry red (or alcohol-free) wine	8 cups	2 L
Corn syrup	⅔ cup	150 mL
Cinnamon sticks, (4 inches, 10 cm, each in length), broken up and crushed in plastic bag	3	3
Whole allspice	1 tsp.	5 mL
Whole cloves	1 tsp.	5 mL
Medium orange, sliced	1	1
Lemon juice	1 tsp.	5 mL
Prepared orange juice (or cranberry cocktail)	2 cups	500 mL

Combine wine and corn syrup in 3½ quart (3.5 L) slow cooker. Stir.

Tie cinnamon, allspice and cloves in double layer of cheesecloth. Add to slow cooker.

Add remaining 3 ingredients. Cover. Cook on Low for at least 3 hours. Discard spice bag. Discard orange slices if desired. Makes 9 cups (2.25 L).

1 cup (250 mL): 267 Calories; 0.1 g Total Fat; 29 mg Sodium; 1 g Protein; 31 g Carbohydrate

1. Dried Fruit Compote, page 78
2. Hot Chocolate, page 55
3. Oatmeal Porridge, page 60
4. Date Loaf, page 63
5. Ham Steaks, page 103
6. Cranberry Loaf, page 64
7. Banana Bread, page 62

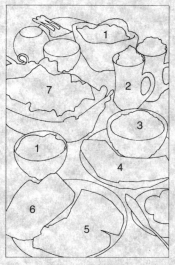

Props Courtesy Of: Creations By Design;
Dansk Gifts; Eaton's;
La Cache; Stokes

MOCHA HOT SPOT

Triple the flavor with coffee, chocolate and liqueur.

Prepared coffee, warm or cold	8 cups	2 L
Sweetened chocolate drink powder	½ cup	125 mL
Powdered coffee whitener	¼ cup	60 mL
Kahlua (or Tia Maria) liqueur	½ cup	125 mL

Frozen whipped topping (in a tub),
   thawed (or whipped cream), optional
Grated chocolate, sprinkle (optional)

Combine first 4 ingredients in 3½ quart (3.5 L) slow cooker. Stir. Cover. Cook on Low for at least 3 hours until hot.

Pour into mugs. Top with a dollop of whipped topping. Sprinkle with chocolate. Makes 8½ cups (2.1 L).

1 cup (250 mL): 110 Calories; 1.4 g Total Fat; 33 mg Sodium; 1 g Protein; 17 g Carbohydrate

HOT CHOCOLATE

Imagine this after a family outing—skating, tobogganing or during a video.

Skim milk powder	4 cups	1 L
Cocoa	¾ cup	175 mL
Icing (confectioner's) sugar	1 cup	250 mL
Water	10 cups	2.5 L

Frozen whipped topping (in a tub),
   thawed (or marshmallows), optional
Grated chocolate (optional)

Combine first 3 ingredients in 3½ quart (3.5 L) slow cooker. Stir well.

Add water. Stir. Cover. Cook on Low for at least 3 hours until hot. Stir. Ladle into mugs.

Top with whipped topping. Sprinkle with chocolate. Makes 11½ cups (2.85 L).

1 cup (250 mL): 213 Calories; 0.9 g Total Fat; 237 mg Sodium; 17 g Protein; 37 g Carbohydrate

Pictured on page 53.

GLÖGG

This beverage is a good tasty variation of the Swedish drink. To make more authentic, add a few raisins and whole almonds to each mug. Brandy or aquavit (a strong colorless Scandinavian liquor) may also be added.

Cardamom seeds, crushed in plastic bag	20	20
Whole cloves	25	25
Cinnamon sticks (4 inches, 10 cm, each in length), broken up and crushed in plastic bag	4	4
Red wine (or alcohol-free wine)	6 cups	1.5 L
Prepared orange juice	1 cup	250 mL
Lemon juice	1/4 cup	60 mL
Granulated sugar	1/2 cup	125 mL

Tie cardamom, cloves and cinnamon in double layer of cheesecloth. Add to 3½ quart (3.5 L) slow cooker.

Add remaining 4 ingredients. Stir. Cover. Cook on Low for at least 3 hours until quite warm. Discard spice bag. Makes 7⅓ cups (1.8 L).

1 cup (250 mL): 220 Calories; trace Total Fat; 11 mg Sodium; 1 g Protein; 22 g Carbohydrate

RED HOT PUNCH

Clear red color with a subtle strawberry flavor.

Water	6 cups	1.5 L
Tropical punch-flavored crystals with sugar	2/3 cup	150 mL
Lemon-lime soft drink (or ginger ale)	3½ cups	875 mL
Lemon juice	1/4 cup	60 mL
Frozen sliced strawberries, in syrup, thawed	15 oz.	425 g

Combine water, flavored crystals, soft drink and lemon juice in 3½ quart (3.5 L) slow cooker.

Add strawberries with syrup. Stir. Cover. Cook on Low for at least 3 hours until quite warm. Remove strawberries with slotted spoon. Discard strawberries. Strain liquid to remove pulp if desired. Makes 10½ cups (2.6 L).

1 cup (250 mL): 126 Calories; 0.1 g Total Fat; 27 mg Sodium; trace Protein; 33 g Carbohydrate

HOT BUTTERED RUM

This toddy is easy to take.

Water	12 cups	3 L
Rum	2 cups	500 mL
Brown sugar, packed	½ cup	125 mL
Hard margarine (or butter)	¼ cup	60 mL
Ground cinnamon	¼ tsp.	1 mL
Ground nutmeg	¼ tsp.	1 mL
Ground cloves	⅛ tsp.	0.5 mL
Salt	1/16 tsp.	0.5 mL

Combine all 8 ingredients in 5 quart (5 L) slow cooker. Stir well. Cover. Cook on Low for at least 3 hours until quite warm. Makes 13 cups (3.25 L).

1 cup (250 mL): 151 Calories; 3.8 g Total Fat; 60 mg Sodium; trace Protein; 9 g Carbohydrate

CRANBERRY WARMER

Mild with a bit of tang. A pick-me-up rosy drink.

Cranberry cocktail	4 cups	1 L
Pineapple juice	4 cups	1 L
Prepared orange juice	2 cups	500 mL
Brown sugar, packed	½ cup	125 mL
Whole cloves	20	20
Cinnamon sticks (4 inch, 10 cm, each in length), broken up and crushed in plastic bag	4	4

Combine first 4 ingredients in 3½ quart (3.5 L) slow cooker. Stir.

Tie cloves and cinnamon in double layer of cheesecloth. Add to slow cooker. Cover. Cook on Low for at least 3 hours until quite warm. Discard spice bag. Makes 10 cups (2.5 L).

Variation: Wine or gin may be added if desired. Use about 2 cups (500 mL) wine or about 1½ cups (375 mL) gin.

1 cup (250 mL): 188 Calories; 0.2 g Total Fat; 9 mg Sodium; 1 g Protein; 47 g Carbohydrate

Pictured on page 17.

WHITE BREAD

This bread has a touch more porous texture with the same homemade aroma and flavor as regular bread. No kneading or rising.

Granulated sugar	2 tsp.	10 mL
Warm water	1¼ cups	300 mL
Envelope active dry yeast	1 x ¼ oz.	1 x 8 g
(1 scant tbsp., 15 mL)		
All-purpose flour	2 cups	500 mL
Granulated sugar	2 tbsp.	30 mL
Cooking oil	2 tbsp.	30 mL
Salt	1 tsp.	5 mL
All-purpose flour	1 cup	250 mL

Stir first amount of sugar and warm water together in large bowl. Sprinkle with yeast. Let stand for 10 minutes. Stir to dissolve yeast.

Add first amount of flour, second amount of sugar, cooking oil and salt. Beat on low to moisten. Beat on high for 2 minutes.

Work in second amount of flour. Grease bottom of 3½ quart (3.5 L) slow cooker. Turn batter into slow cooker. Lay 5 paper towels between top of slow cooker and lid. Put wooden match or an object ⅛ inch (3 mm) thick between paper towels and edge of slow cooker to allow a bit of steam to escape. Do not lift lid for the first 1¾ hours cooking time. Cook on High for about 2 hours. Loosen sides with knife. Turn out onto rack to cool. Cuts into 16 slices.

1 slice: 115 Calories; 2 g Total Fat; 170 mg Sodium; 3 g Protein; 21 g Carbohydrate

Pictured on front cover.

BROWN QUICK BREAD

A porous biscuit-like mealtime or coffee break treat.

Whole wheat flour	2 cups	500 mL
All-purpose flour	1 cup	250 mL
Baking powder	1 tbsp.	15 mL
Salt	1 tsp.	5 mL
Molasses (not blackstrap)	2 tbsp.	30 mL
Cooking oil	2 tbsp.	30 mL
Water	1⅓ cups	325 mL

(continued on next page)

Combine first 4 ingredients in bowl. Stir.

Add molasses, cooking oil and water. Mix until moistened. Turn into greased 5 quart (5 L) slow cooker. Place 5 paper towels between top of slow cooker and lid. Put wooden match or an object ⅛ inch (3 mm) thick between paper towels and edge of slow cooker to allow a bit of steam to escape. Do not lift lid for the first 1¾ hours cooking time. Cook on High for about 2 hours. Loosen sides with knife. Turn out onto rack to cool. Cuts into 14 wedges.

1 wedge: 122 Calories; 2.4 g Total Fat; 200 mg Sodium; 3 g Protein; 22 g Carbohydrate

TOMATO HERB BREAD

This gets its color from the tomato sauce.

Granulated sugar	1 tsp.	5 mL
Warm water	⅓ cup	75 mL
Envelope active dry yeast	1 × ¼ oz.	1 × 8 g
(1 scant tbsp., 15 mL)		
All-purpose flour	2 cups	500 mL
Granulated sugar	1 tbsp.	15 mL
Finely minced onion	¼ cup	60 mL
Lukewarm tomato sauce, plus water	7.5 oz.	213 mL
to make 1 cup (250 mL)		
Grated sharp Cheddar cheese	¼ cup	60 mL
Salt	1 tsp.	5 mL
Pepper	¼ tsp.	1 mL
Dried whole oregano	½ tsp.	2 mL
All-purpose flour	1 cup	250 mL

Stir first amount of sugar into warm water in large warmed bowl. Sprinkle yeast over top. Let stand for 10 minutes. Stir to dissolve yeast.

Add next 8 ingredients. Beat on low to moisten. Beat on high for 2 minutes.

Work in second amount of flour. Turn into greased 3½ quart (3.5 L) slow cooker. Smooth top with wet spoon or hand. Place 5 paper towels between top of slow cooker and lid. Put wooden match or an object ⅛ inch (3 mm) thick between paper towels and edge of slow cooker to allow a bit of steam to escape. Do not lift lid for the first 2 hours cooking time. Cook on High for about 2½ hours. Loosen sides with knife. Turn out onto rack to cool. Cuts into 14 slices.

1 slice: 124 Calories; 1 g Total Fat; 303 mg Sodium; 4 g Protein; 25 g Carbohydrate

Pictured on page 89.

PUMPERNICKEL BREAD

Dark colored, aromatic and so good. No pre-rising to this.

Granulated sugar	1 tsp.	5 mL
Warm water	1⅓ cups	325 mL
Envelope active dry yeast	1 × ¼ oz.	1 × 8 g
(1 scant tbsp.,15 mL)		
All-purpose flour	1 cup	250 mL
Rye flour	1 cup	250 mL
Molasses (not blackstrap)	2 tbsp.	30 mL
Cooking oil	2 tbsp.	30 mL
Cocoa	2 tbsp.	30 mL
Salt	1 tsp.	5 mL
Caraway seed (optional)	2 tsp.	10 mL
Rye flour	1 cup	250 mL

Stir sugar into warm water in large bowl. Sprinkle yeast over top. Let stand for 10 minutes. Stir to dissolve yeast.

Add next 7 ingredients. Beat on low to moisten. Beat on high for 2 minutes.

Stir in second amount of rye flour. Grease bottom of 3½ quart (3.5 L) slow cooker. Turn dough into cooker. Lay 5 paper towels between top of slow cooker and lid. Put wooden match or an object ⅛ inch (3 mm) thick between paper towels and edge of slow cooker to allow a bit of steam to escape. Do not lift lid for the first 1¾ hours cooking time. Cook on High for about 2 hours. Loosen sides with knife. Turn out onto rack to cool. Cuts into 14 slices.

1 slice: 118 Calories; 2.4 g Total Fat; 196 mg Sodium; 3 g Protein; 22 g Carbohydrate; good source of Dietary Fiber

Pictured on front cover.

OATMEAL PORRIDGE

This will wait for you, even if your overnight is a bit longer. Serve with cream and sugar.

Large flake rolled oats (old-fashioned)	2½ cups	625 mL
Water	5 cups	1.25 L
Salt	½ tsp.	2 mL

Mix all 3 ingredients in 3½ quart (3.5 L) slow cooker. Cover. Cook on Low for 7 to 8 hours overnight. Makes 5½ cups (1.3 L).

¾ cup (175 mL): 105 Calories; 1.7 g Total Fat; 174 mg Sodium; 4 g Protein; 18 g Carbohydrate

Pictured on page 53.

Nicely rounded loaf. Herb colored with good flavor.

Granulated sugar	1 tsp.	5 mL
Warm water	1⅓ cups	325 mL
Envelope active dry yeast	1 × ¼ oz.	1 × 8 g
(1 scant tbsp., 15 mL)		
All-purpose flour	2 cups	500 mL
Granulated sugar	1 tbsp.	15 mL
Cooking oil	2 tbsp.	30 mL
Dried whole oregano	1 tsp.	5 mL
Ground sage	1 tsp.	5 mL
Garlic powder	¼ tsp.	1 mL
Onion powder	¼ tsp.	1 mL
Salt	1 tsp.	5 mL
All-purpose flour	1 cup	250 mL

Stir first amount of sugar in warm water in large warmed bowl. Sprinkle with yeast. Let stand for 10 minutes. Stir to dissolve yeast.

Add next 8 ingredients. Beat on low to moisten. Beat on medium for 2 minutes.

Work in second amount of flour. Turn into greased 3½ quart (3.5 L) slow cooker. Smooth top with wet spoon or hand. Place 5 paper towels between top of slow cooker and lid. Put wooden match or an object ⅛ inch (3 mm) thick between paper towels and edge of slow cooker to allow a bit of steam to escape. Do not lift lid for the first 2 hours cooking time. Cook on High for about 2½ hours. Loosen sides with knife. Turn out onto rack to cool. Cuts into 14 slices.

1 slice: 128 Calories; 2.3 g Total Fat; 195 mg Sodium; 3 g Protein; 23 g Carbohydrate

Pictured on page 71.

Paré Pointer

If your dog's tail gets in the lawn mower, you will have to take him to a retail store.

BANANA BREAD

Makes a large dark loaf. Good flavor. Serve plain or buttered.

Hard margarine (or butter), softened	6 tbsp.	100 mL
Granulated sugar	²/₃ cup	150 mL
Large egg	1	1
Mashed banana (about 3 small)	³/₄ cup	175 mL
All-purpose flour	1¹/₂ cups	375 mL
Cocoa	1 tbsp.	15 mL
Baking powder	1¹/₂ tsp.	7 mL
Baking soda	¹/₄ tsp.	1 mL
Salt	¹/₂ tsp.	2 mL
Chopped walnuts (optional)	¹/₂ cup	125 mL

Cream margarine and sugar together in bowl. Beat in eggs, 1 at a time. Add banana. Mix.

Add remaining 6 ingredients. Stir to moisten. Turn into greased 9 x 5 x 3 inch (22 x 12 x 7.5 cm) loaf pan. Set pan on wire trivet in 5 quart (5 L) oval slow cooker. Place 5 paper towels between top of slow cooker and lid. Put wooden match or an object ¹/₈ inch (3 mm) thick between paper towels and edge of slow cooker to allow a bit of steam to escape. Do not lift lid for the first 2 hours cooking time. Cook on High for about 2¹/₄ hours. A wooden pick inserted in center should come out clean. Remove pan to wire rack to cool. Let stand for 20 minutes. Loosen sides with knife. Turn out onto rack to cool. Cuts into 18 slices.

1 slice: 118 Calories; 4.2 g Total Fat; 144 mg Sodium; 2 g Protein; 19 g Carbohydrate

Pictured on page 53.

In reality, a pirate ship is a thug boat.

A large moist loaf. Spread with butter—delicious.

Boiling water	⅔ **cup**	**150 mL**
Baking soda	**1 tsp.**	**5 mL**
Chopped dates	**1 cup**	**250 mL**
Large egg, fork-beaten	**1**	**1**
Granulated sugar	⅔ **cup**	**150 mL**
Hard margarine (or butter), melted	**2 tbsp.**	**30 mL**
Vanilla	½ **tsp.**	**2 mL**
Salt	¼ **tsp.**	**1 mL**
All-purpose flour	1⅔ **cups**	**400 mL**
Chopped walnuts	½ **cup**	**125 mL**

Pour boiling water over baking soda in bowl. Stir. Add dates. Stir. Let stand until cool.

Combine egg, sugar, margarine, vanilla and salt in separate bowl. Beat. Add date mixture. Stir.

Add flour and walnuts. Stir. Turn into greased 9 x 5 x 3 inch (22 x 12 x 7.5 cm) loaf pan. Place pan on wire trivet in 5 quart (5 L) oval slow cooker. Place 5 paper towels between top of slow cooker and lid. Put wooden match or an object ⅛ inch (3 mm) thick between paper towels and edge of slow cooker to allow a bit of steam to escape. Do not lift lid for the first 2 hours cooking time. Cook on High for about 2¾ hours until wooden pick inserted in center comes out clean. Remove pan to rack. Let stand for 20 minutes. Loosen sides with knife. Turn out onto rack to cool. Cuts into 18 slices.

1 slice: 138 Calories; 4 g Total Fat; 134 mg Sodium; 2 g Protein; 24 g Carbohydrate

Pictured on page 53.

Paré Pointer

Is butter a young goat?

CRANBERRY LOAF

Lots of flavor and most colorful slices.

Large egg	1	1
Prepared orange juice	²/₃ cup	150 mL
Hard margarine (or butter), melted	2 tbsp.	30 mL
Granulated sugar	1 cup	250 mL
Salt	1 tsp.	5 mL
Vanilla	¹/₂ tsp.	2 mL
All-purpose flour	2 cups	500 mL
Baking powder	1¹/₂ tsp.	7 mL
Coarsely chopped fresh (or frozen, thawed) cranberries	1 cup	250 mL

Beat egg in bowl. Add next 5 ingredients. Beat until smooth.

Add flour and baking powder. Stir just to moisten.

Add cranberries. Stir lightly. Turn into greased 9 x 5 x 3 inch (22 x 12 x 7.5 cm) loaf pan. Set pan on wire trivet in 5 quart (5 L) oval slow cooker. Place 5 paper towels between top of slow cooker and lid. Put wooden match between paper towels and edge of slow cooker to allow a bit of steam to escape. Cook on High for about 2¹/₂ hours until wooden pick inserted in center comes out clean. Remove pan from slow cooker. Let stand for 20 minutes. Loosen sides with knife. Turn out onto rack to cool. Cuts into 18 slices.

1 slice: 122 Calories; 1.8 g Total Fat; 171 mg Sodium; 2 g Protein; 25 g Carbohydrate

Pictured on page 53.

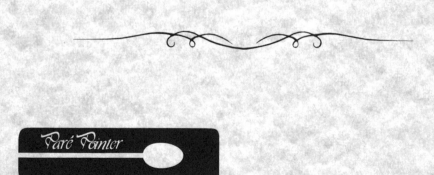

Paré Pointer

It is always the last place you look that you find what you're looking for. Naturally. Why else would you keep looking?

A handy cake mix and applesauce combine to make this spicy cake.

Yellow cake mix (2 layer size)	1	1
Instant vanilla pudding (4 serving size)	1	1
Ground cinnamon	½ tsp.	2 mL
Ground nutmeg	¼ tsp.	1 mL
Ground allspice	¼ tsp.	1 mL
Large eggs, fork-beaten	4	4
Canned applesauce	14 oz.	398 mL

Butterscotch Icing, page 68,
 double recipe

Place first 7 ingredients in bowl. Beat on low to moisten. Beat on medium for 2 minutes until smooth. Line greased 5 quart (5 L) round slow cooker with foil. Pour batter over foil. Place 5 paper towels between top of slow cooker and lid. Put wooden match or an object ⅛ inch (3 mm) thick between paper towels and edge of slow cooker to allow a bit of steam to escape. Do not lift lid for at least 2 hours. Cook on High for 2½ hours until wooden pick inserted in center comes out clean. Remove slow cooker liner to rack or turn slow cooker off. Let stand for 20 minutes. Loosen sides of cake with knife. Invert cake onto plate, foil side up, then onto rack, foil side down, to cool. Remove foil before serving.

Cut cake into 2 layers if desired. Ice with Butterscotch Icing. Cuts into 12 wedges.

1 wedge: 464 Calories; 13.1 g Total Fat; 296 mg Sodium; 4 g Protein; 85 g Carbohydrate

Pictured on page 71.

Paré Pointer

It is odd how both a goose and an icicle grow down.

CARROT CAKE

Can be a one or two-layer cake.

Yellow cake mix (2 layer size)	1	1
Ground cinnamon	1½ tsp.	7 mL
Ground nutmeg	½ tsp.	2 mL
Grated carrot	1½ cups	375 mL
Large eggs	3	3
Cooking oil	⅓ cup	75 mL
Water	½ cup	125 mL
CREAM CHEESE ICING		
Cream cheese, softened	4 oz.	125 g
Hard margarine (or butter), softened	2 tbsp.	30 mL
Vanilla	1 tsp.	5 mL
Icing (confectioner's) sugar	2 cups	500 mL

Combine cake mix, cinnamon, nutmeg and carrot in bowl. Mix.

Add eggs, cooking oil and water. Beat on low until moistened. Beat on medium for 2 minutes. Line bottom of 5 quart (5 L) round slow cooker with foil. Pour cake batter over top. Place 5 paper towels between top of slow cooker and lid. Put wooden match or an object ⅛ inch (3 mm) thick between paper towels and edge of slow cooker to allow a bit of steam to escape. Do not lift lid. Cook on High for about 2 hours until wooden pick inserted in center comes out clean. Remove slow cooker liner to rack or turn slow cooker off. Let stand for about 20 minutes. Loosen sides of cake with knife. Invert cake onto plate, foil side up, then onto rack, foil side down, to cool. Remove foil before serving. Slice into 2 layers or leave as is.

Cream Cheese Icing: Beat all 4 ingredients together in bowl until smooth. Makes about 1¾ cups (425 mL). Ice top and sides of cake. Cuts into 12 wedges.

1 wedge: 402 Calories; 18.8 g Total Fat; 248 mg Sodium; 4 g Protein; 56 g Carbohydrate

Pictured on page 89.

Paré Pointer

It is said that the first few missionaries gave the cannibals their first taste of Christianity.

The crowning glory is the pink raspberry icing.

Chocolate cake mix (2 layer size), see Note	1	1
FILLING		
Raspberry (or strawberry) jam	1 cup	250 mL
RASPBERRY ICING		
Hard margarine (or butter), softened	6 tbsp.	100 mL
Raspberry unsweetened drink powder	1 tsp.	5 mL
Icing (confectioner's) sugar	1½ cups	375 mL
Water	¼ cup	60 mL
Icing (confectioner's) sugar	1½ cups	375 mL

Prepare cake mix as directed on package. Line bottom of 5 quart (5 L) round slow cooker with foil. Pour batter over foil. Place 5 paper towels between top of slow cooker and lid. Put wooden match or an object ⅛ inch (3 mm) thick between paper towels and edge of slow cooker to allow a bit of steam to escape. Do not lift lid for at least 2 hours. Cook on High for about 2½ hours until wooden pick inserted in center comes out clean. Remove slow cooker liner to rack or turn slow cooker off. Let stand, uncovered, for 20 minutes. Loosen sides of cake with knife. Invert cake onto plate, foil side up, then onto rack, foil side down, to cool. Remove foil before serving.

Filling: Cut cake into 2 layers. Spread bottom layer with jam. Place second layer on top.

Raspberry Icing: Measure first 4 ingredients into bowl. Beat until creamy.

Add second amount of icing sugar. Beat well. Add more water or icing sugar if needed to make proper spreading consistency. Makes 2 cups (500 mL). Ice top and sides of cake. Cuts into 12 wedges.

Note: Testing showed that white or yellow cake mixes could not be substituted.

1 wedge: 424 Calories; 10.5 g Total Fat; 309 mg Sodium; 2 g Protein; 84 g Carbohydrate

Pictured on front cover.

"SCRATCH" CHOCOLATE CAKE: Combine 1 chocolate cake mix, 1 chocolate or vanilla instant pudding (4 serving size), 4 eggs, ½ cup (125 mL) cooking oil and 1 cup (250 mL) water. Mix and cook as for Chocolate Cake, above.

GRAHAM CRUMB CAKE

This is such a neat cake. The graham crumbs take the place of flour. Chewy texture.

Hard margarine (or butter), softened	½ cup	125 mL
Granulated sugar	¾ cup	175 mL
Large eggs	2	2
Graham cracker crumbs	2¼ cups	560 mL
Medium coconut	½ cup	125 mL
Baking powder	1½ tsp.	7 mL
Salt	⅛ tsp.	0.5 mL
Milk	½ cup	125 mL
Vanilla	1 tsp.	5 mL
BUTTERSCOTCH ICING		
Brown sugar, packed	6 tbsp.	100 mL
Milk (or cream)	2½ tbsp.	37 mL
Hard margarine (or butter)	3 tbsp.	50 mL
Icing (confectioner's) sugar	1¼ cups	300 mL

Cream margarine and sugar together in bowl. Beat in eggs, 1 at a time. Add graham crumbs, coconut, baking powder and salt. Stir well.

Add milk and vanilla. Stir. Line bottom of greased 5 quart (5 L) round slow cooker with foil. Pour batter over foil. Place 5 paper towels between top of slow cooker and lid. Put wooden match or an object ⅛ inch (3 mm) thick between paper towels and edge of slow cooker to allow a bit of steam to escape. Do not lift lid. Cook on High for 2 hours until wooden pick inserted in center comes out clean. Remove slow cooker liner to rack or turn slow cooker off. Let stand for 20 minutes. Loosen sides of cake with knife. Invert cake onto plate, foil side up, then onto rack, foil side down, to cool. Remove foil before serving.

Butterscotch Icing: Combine brown sugar, milk and margarine in saucepan. Heat and stir until boiling. Boil for 2 minutes. Remove from heat. Cool.

Add icing sugar. Beat until smooth, adding more milk or icing sugar, if needed, to make proper spreading consistency. Makes about 1 cup (250 mL). Ice top and sides of cake. Cuts into 12 wedges.

1 wedge: 354 Calories; 16.7 g Total Fat; 327 mg Sodium; 4 g Protein; 51 g Carbohydrate

Maple Whip Icing dresses up any cake.

Yellow cake mix (2 layer size)	1	1
Instant vanilla pudding (4 serving size)	1	1
Water	1 cup	250 mL
Rum flavoring	1 tbsp.	15 mL
Large eggs	4	4
MAPLE WHIP ICING		
Envelope unflavored gelatin	1 x ¼ oz.	1 x 7 g
Water	¼ cup	60 mL
Brown sugar, packed	¼ cup	60 mL
Envelopes dessert topping (not prepared)	2	2
Milk	1 cup	250 mL
Maple flavoring	1 tsp.	5 mL

Combine first 5 ingredients in bowl. Beat on low to moisten. Beat on medium for 2 minutes until smooth. Line greased 5 quart (5 L) round slow cooker with foil. Pour batter over foil. Place 5 paper towels between top of slow cooker and lid. Put wooden match or an object ⅛ inch (3 mm) thick between paper towels and edge of slow cooker to allow a bit of steam to escape. Cook on High for about 2½ hours until wooden pick inserted in center comes out clean. Remove slow cooker liner to rack or turn slow cooker off. Let stand for 20 minutes. Loosen sides of cake with knife. Invert cake onto plate, foil side up, then onto rack, foil side down, to cool. Remove foil before serving.

Maple Whip Icing: Sprinkle gelatin over water in small saucepan. Let stand for 1 minute.

Add brown sugar. Heat and stir to dissolve. Cool.

Beat dessert topping, milk and maple flavoring together according to package directions until soft peaks form. Add gelatin mixture. Beat until stiff. Makes 4⅔ cups (1.15 L) icing. Cut cake into 2 or 3 layers. Fill and ice top and sides of cake. Cuts into 12 wedges.

1 wedge: 314 Calories; 10.2 g Total Fat; 241 mg Sodium; 5 g Protein; 51 g Carbohydrate

CHERRY WHIP ICING: Omit brown sugar and maple flavoring. Add ½ cup (125 mL) or more chopped maraschino cherries and 1 tsp. (5 mL) each of vanilla and almond flavoring.

STEAMED FRUIT PUDDING

Serve with your favorite pudding sauce. A carefree method for cooking a fruit pudding.

Hard margarine (or butter), softened	³/₄ cup	175 mL
Granulated sugar	³/₄ cup	175 mL
Large eggs	2	2
Prepared orange (or apple) juice	¹/₂ cup	125 mL
Raisins	2 cups	500 mL
Cut mixed glazed fruit	1¹/₂ cups	375 mL
Fine dry bread crumbs	1 cup	250 mL
Ground cinnamon	1 tsp.	5 mL
Ground allspice	¹/₂ tsp.	2 mL
Baking powder	³/₄ tsp.	4 mL
Baking soda	¹/₂ tsp.	2 mL
Salt	1 tsp.	5 mL
All-purpose flour	1 cup	250 mL

Cream margarine and sugar together in bowl. Beat in eggs, 1 at a time. Add orange juice. Beat.

Combine remaining 9 ingredients in separate large bowl. Stir together well. Pour orange juice mixture into dry ingredients. Stir until moistened. Turn into greased 8 cup (2 L) pudding pan. Cover with greased foil, tying sides down with string. Place on wire trivet in 5 quart (5 L) slow cooker. Pour boiling water into slow cooker to reach halfway up sides of pudding pan. Cover. Cook on High for 5 hours. Serves 16.

1 serving: 311 Calories; 10.4 g Total Fat; 397 mg Sodium; 3 g Protein; 54 g Carbohydrate

1. Borscht, page 141
2. Herb Bread, page 61
3. Asparagus Bake, page 148
4. Poached Salmon, page 84
5. Glazed Ham, page 102
6. Apple Cake, page 65, with
   Butterscotch Icing, page 68

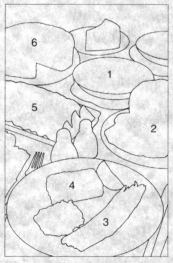

Props Courtesy Of: La Cache; Stokes; The Bay; Tile Town Ltd.

RICE PUDDING

Serve hot or cold. Ice cream or cream finishes this nicely.

Uncooked short grain white rice	¾ cup	175 mL
Skim evaporated milk	13½ oz.	385 mL
Water	2 cups	500 mL
Granulated sugar	⅓ cup	75 mL
Raisins	½ cup	125 mL
Vanilla	1½ tsp.	7 mL
Salt	¾ tsp.	4 mL
Cinnamon stick (3 inches, 7.5 cm, in length)	1	1

Measure all 8 ingredients into 3½ quart (3.5 L) slow cooker. Stir. Cover. Cook on Low for 4 to 5 hours or on High for 2 to 2½ hours, stirring once or twice. Makes 4¾ cups (1.2 L).

1 cup (250 mL): 298 Calories; 0.4 g Total Fat; 532 mg Sodium; 9 g Protein; 64 g Carbohydrate

STEAMED CHOCOLATE PUDDING

No egg in this. Makes a chewy brownie-like dessert. Serve with ice cream and chocolate sauce.

Hard margarine (or butter), softened	1 tbsp.	15 mL
Granulated sugar	½ cup	125 mL
Cocoa	2 tbsp.	30 mL
Milk	½ cup	125 mL
Vanilla	½ tsp.	2 mL
All-purpose flour	1½ cups	375 mL
Baking powder	2 tsp.	10 mL
Salt	½ tsp.	2 mL

Boiling water, to cover

Cream margarine, sugar, and cocoa together in bowl. Add milk and vanilla. Beat well.

Add flour, baking powder and salt. Mix well. Turn into greased 4 cup (1 L) bowl. Cover with greased foil, tying sides down with string. Place wire trivet in 5 quart (5 L) or 6 quart (6 L) slow cooker. Set bowl on top.

Pour boiling water into slow cooker to reach halfway up bowl. Cover. Cook on High for 2½ hours. Serves 6.

1 serving: 221 Calories; 2.7 g Total Fat; 266 mg Sodium; 5 g Protein; 45 g Carbohydrate

PEACH PUDDING

Serve warm with ice cream. A mild spicy flavor.

All-purpose flour	1 cup	250 mL
Granulated sugar	½ cup	125 mL
Brown sugar, packed	¼ cup	60 mL
Baking powder	2 tsp.	10 mL
Salt	½ tsp.	2 mL
Ground cinnamon	½ tsp.	2 mL
Ground nutmeg	¼ tsp.	1 mL
Large eggs, fork-beaten	2	2
Cooking oil	2 tbsp.	30 mL
Vanilla	1 tsp.	5 mL
Milk	1⅛ cups	280 mL
Canned sliced peaches, drained and chopped	14 oz.	398 mL

Measure first 7 ingredients into bowl. Stir.

Add eggs, cooking oil, vanilla and milk. Mix well.

Stir in peaches. Turn into greased 3½ quart (3.5 L) slow cooker. Place 5 paper towels between top of slow cooker and lid. Cook on High for about 2 hours until wooden pick inserted in center comes out clean. Serves 6.

1 serving: 292 Calories; 7.1 g Total Fat; 282 mg Sodium; 6 g Protein; 51 g Carbohydrate

LEMON-SAUCED PUDDING

A yummy lemon flavor. A cake-like top with lemon sauce to spoon over. Serve with ice cream.

All-purpose flour	1 cup	250 mL
Granulated sugar	½ cup	125 mL
Baking powder	2 tsp.	10 mL
Grated lemon peel	2 tsp.	10 mL
Salt	⅛ tsp.	0.5 mL
Milk	½ cup	125 mL
Cooking oil	2 tbsp.	30 mL
Hot water	1¾ cups	425 mL
Lemon juice	¼ cup	60 mL
Granulated sugar	¾ cup	175 mL

(continued on next page)

Measure first 7 ingredients into bowl. Mix well. Turn into greased 3½ quart (3.5 L) slow cooker.

Stir hot water, lemon juice and second amount of sugar together in separate bowl. Pour carefully over batter. Do not stir. Place 5 paper towels between top of slow cooker and lid. Cook on High for about 2 hours until wooden pick inserted in center comes out clean. Makes 6 small servings.

1 serving: 304 Calories; 5.1 g Total Fat; 76 mg Sodium; 3 g Protein; 63 g Carbohydrate

BUMBLEBERRY COBBLER

Fruity and warm. Serve with ice cream to top it off.

All-purpose flour	1 cup	250 mL
Granulated sugar	½ cup	125 mL
Baking powder	1½ tsp.	7 mL
Ground cinnamon	½ tsp.	2 mL
Salt	½ tsp.	2 mL
Large eggs, fork-beaten	2	2
Cooking oil	2 tbsp.	30 mL
Milk	2 tbsp.	30 mL
Vanilla	1 tsp.	5 mL
Fresh (or frozen) raspberries	1 cup	250 mL
Fresh (or frozen) blueberries	1 cup	250 mL
Sliced fresh (or whole frozen, sliced) strawberries	1 cup	250 mL
Granulated sugar	¾ cup	175 mL
Water	½ cup	125 mL

Stir first 5 ingredients together in bowl.

Add eggs, cooking oil, milk and vanilla. Mix well. Turn into ungreased 3½ quart (3.5 L) slow cooker.

Measure remaining 5 ingredients into saucepan. Heat, stirring occasionally, until boiling. Pour over batter in slow cooker. Place 5 paper towels between top of slow cooker and lid. Cook on High for 1¾ to 2 hours. Serves 6.

1 serving: 353 Calories; 6.9 g Total Fat; 255 mg Sodium; 5 g Protein; 69 g Carbohydrate; good source of Dietary Fiber

QUICK MIX PUDDING

A cinnamon-raisin treat with plenty of butterscotch sauce to top it off.

All-purpose flour	1 cup	250 mL
Granulated sugar	2/3 cup	150 mL
Baking powder	2 tsp.	10 mL
Ground cinnamon	1/2 tsp.	2 mL
Salt	1/8 tsp.	0.5 mL
Milk	1/2 cup	125 mL
Cooking oil	2 tbsp.	30 mL
Raisins (or currants)	1/2 cup	125 mL
Vanilla	1/2 tsp.	2 mL
Brown sugar, packed	3/4 cup	175 mL
Vanilla	1/2 tsp.	2 mL
Hot water	1 3/4 cups	425 mL

Stir first 5 ingredients in bowl.

Add milk, cooking oil, raisins and first amount of vanilla. Mix well. Turn into 3½ quart (3.5 L) slow cooker.

Stir brown sugar, second amount of vanilla and hot water together in bowl. Pour carefully over batter in slow cooker. Do not stir. Cover. Cook on High for about 2 hours until wooden pick inserted in center comes out clean. Serves 4 to 6.

1/4 recipe: 559 Calories; 7.7 g Total Fat; 129 mg Sodium; 5 g Protein; 120 g Carbohydrate

BROWN BETTY

Looks and tastes just like Brown Betty.

Medium cooking apples, peeled, cored and sliced (such as McIntosh)	4	4
Brown sugar, packed	3/4 cup	175 mL
Quick-cooking rolled oats (not instant)	1/3 cup	75 mL
All-purpose flour	1/2 cup	125 mL
Salt	1/4 tsp.	1 mL
Hard margarine (or butter), softened	1/3 cup	75 mL

(continued on next page)

Place apple slices in 3½ quart (3.5 L) slow cooker.

Mix remaining 5 ingredients in bowl until crumbly. Sprinkle over apple. Place 5 paper towels between top of slow cooker and lid. Put wooden match between paper towels and edge of slow cooker to allow a bit of steam to escape. Cook on High for 1½ to 2 hours. Serves 4.

1 cup (250 mL): 468 Calories; 17.2 g Total Fat; 374 mg Sodium; 3 g Protein; 79 g Carbohydrate; good source of Dietary Fiber

CHOCOLATE FUDGE PUDDING

No need to heat up the kitchen to enjoy this yummy dessert. Good chocolate flavor with lots of sauce.

All-purpose flour	1 cup	250 mL
Brown sugar, packed	¾ cup	175 mL
Cocoa	2 tbsp.	30 mL
Baking powder	2 tsp.	10 mL
Salt	¼ tsp.	1 mL
Milk	½ cup	125 mL
Cooking oil	2 tbsp.	30 mL
Vanilla	½ tsp.	2 mL
Brown sugar, packed	¾ cup	175 mL
Cocoa	2 tbsp.	30 mL
Hot water	1¾ cups	425 mL

Place first 5 ingredients in bowl. Stir.

Add milk, cooking oil and vanilla. Stir well. Turn into 3½ quart (3.5 L) slow cooker.

Stir second amount of brown sugar and second amount of cocoa together well in bowl. Add hot water. Mix. Pour carefully over batter in slow cooker. Do not stir. Cover. Cook on High for about 2 hours until wooden pick inserted in center comes out clean. Serves 6.

1 serving: 358 Calories; 5.4 g Total Fat; 148 mg Sodium; 4 g Protein; 77 g Carbohydrate

Paré Pointer

Little Susie ate T.N.T. so her hair would grow bangs.

STEWED RHUBARB

This uses frozen rhubarb which takes a long time on Low to start to cook. Just fix it and forget it.

Frozen cut rhubarb	8 cups	2 L
Granulated sugar	1½ cups	375 mL
Water	½ cup	125 mL

Place rhubarb, sugar and water in 3½ quart (3.5 L) slow cooker. Cover. Cook on Low for 6 to 7 hours. Makes 6 cups (1.5 L).

STEWED STRAWBERRY RHUBARB: Substitute 4 cups (1 L) frozen strawberries for 4 cups (1 L) frozen rhubarb.

½ cup (125 mL): 182 Calories; 0.2 g Total Fat; 3 mg Sodium; 1 g Protein; 47 g Carbohydrate

STEWED PRUNES

Worry-free. Juice doesn't have a chance of boiling away as it does on a burner.

Dried pitted prunes	1 lb.	454 g
Water	3 cups	750 mL

Combine prunes and water in 3½ quart (3.5 L) slow cooker. Cover. Cook on Low for 4 to 5 hours or on High for 2 to 2½ hours. Stir. Makes 4¼ cups (1 L).

½ cup (125 mL): 145 Calories; 0.3 g Total Fat; 2 mg Sodium; 2 g Protein; 38 g Carbohydrate; good source of Dietary Fiber

DRIED FRUIT COMPOTE

A good breakfast dish or light dessert.

Dried pitted prunes	8 oz.	225 g
Dried apricots, halved	8 oz.	225 g
Canned sliced peaches, with juice	2 × 14 oz.	2 × 398 mL
Maraschino cherries	12	12
Water	1½ cups	375 mL
Granulated sugar	½ cup	125 mL

Combine all 6 ingredients in 3½ quart (3.5 L) slow cooker. Stir. Cover. Cook on Low for 3½ to 4 hours. Makes 6¾ cups (1.68 L).

½ cup (125 mL): 142 Calories; 0.2 g Total Fat; 5 mg Sodium; 1 g Protein; 37 g Carbohydrate; good source of Dietary Fiber

Pictured on page 53.

STEWED PEARS

Wonderful pear flavor. Cloves add just a bit of zip. Great for brunch or dessert.

Apple juice	**1½ cups**	**375 mL**
Granulated sugar	**½ cup**	**125 mL**
Lemon juice	**1 tbsp.**	**15 mL**
Whole cloves	**2**	**2**
Fresh pears (such as Bosc), peeled,	**4**	**4**
cored and thinly sliced (see Note)		

Stir apple juice, sugar, lemon juice and cloves together in 3½ quart (3.5 L) slow cooker.

Add pears. Cover. Cook on Low for 6 to 7 hours or on High for 3 to 3½ hours. Makes 3¾ cups (925 mL).

Note: If using bartlett pears, check for doneness sooner as they soften quickly. The same applies to canned pears. Double cloves for shorter stewing time.

½ cup (125 mL): 104 Calories; 0.1 g Total Fat; 4 mg Sodium; trace Protein; 27 g Carbohydrate

APPLESAUCE

May be served hot or cold.

Medium cooking apples (such as	**8**	**8**
McIntosh), peeled, cored and sliced		
Water	**½ cup**	**125 mL**
Granulated sugar (see Note)	**½ cup**	**125 mL**

Combine apple and water in 5 quart (5 L) slow cooker. Cover. Cook on Low for 4½ to 5 hours or on High for 2¼ to 2½ hours until apple is soft.

Sprinkle sugar over top. Stir. Makes a generous 4 cups (1 L).

½ cup (125 mL): 124 Calories; 0.4 g Total Fat; trace Sodium; trace Protein; 32 g Carbohydrate

Note: The amount of sugar will vary, depending on sweetness of apple. Add more or less to desired sweetness.

Pictured on page 17.

Variation: No need to peel or core the apples. Just nip out blossom end, and cut up. Press through food mill when cooked. Makes a smooth applesauce.

MARBLED CHEESECAKE

A perfect dessert to make when your oven is already in use.

GRAHAM CRUST		
Hard margarine (or butter)	4 tsp.	20 mL
Graham cracker crumbs	1/3 cup	75 mL
Granulated sugar	1 tsp.	5 mL

FILLING		
Semisweet chocolate baking squares, cut up	3 x 1 oz.	3 x 28 g
Light cream cheese, softened	12 oz.	375 g
Granulated sugar	3/4 cup	175 mL
Non-fat plain yogurt	1/3 cup	75 mL
Vanilla	1 tsp.	5 mL
Large eggs	4	4
All-purpose flour	1/2 cup	125 mL

Graham Crust: Melt margarine in saucepan. Stir in graham crumbs and sugar. Press in ungreased 8 inch (20 cm) round cake pan.

Filling: Melt chocolate in saucepan over low, stirring often.

Beat cream cheese, sugar, yogurt and vanilla together in large bowl until smooth. Beat in eggs, 1 at a time. Add flour. Mix. Reserve 1 3/4 cups (425 mL) of cheese mixture. Pour remaining cheese mixture over bottom crust.

Stir melted chocolate into reserved 1 3/4 cups (425 mL) of cheese mixture. Stir. Drizzle over top of white layer. Cut through in a zig-zag motion to get a marbled look.

Tear off a 16 inch (40 cm) long piece of foil to make a foil strap. Fold lengthwise to make a strip 16 inches (40 cm) long and 4 inches (10 cm) wide. Set cake pan on center of foil strap. Put wire trivet in bottom of 5 quart (5 L) round slow cooker.

Using foil strap, carefully lower pan into slow cooker, leaving foil strap in the slow cooker to use to remove pan when baking is complete. Place 5 paper towels between top of slow cooker and lid. Cook on High for 3 hours. Remove pan. Cool. Refrigerate for several hours or overnight. Cuts into 12 wedges.

1 wedge: 226 Calories; 11 g Total Fat; 362 mg Sodium; 7 g Protein; 26 g Carbohydrate

Pictured on page 107.

Contains ham, chicken and shrimp as well as vegetables. A full meal dish from the Deep South.

Chopped onion	1½ cups	375 mL
Chopped celery	½ cup	125 mL
Canned tomatoes, with juice, broken up	14 oz.	398 mL
Medium green pepper, chopped	1	1
Cubed smoked ham	1 cup	250 mL
Boneless, skinless chicken breast halves, chopped	2	2
Beef bouillon powder	1½ tsp.	7 mL
Hot water	1 cup	250 mL
Garlic clove (or ¼ tsp., 1 mL, garlic powder)	1	1
Dried whole oregano	½ tsp.	2 mL
Dried sweet basil	½ tsp.	2 mL
Salt	½ tsp.	2 mL
Pepper	¼ tsp.	1 mL
Cayenne pepper	¼ tsp.	1 mL
Parsley flakes	2 tsp.	10 mL
Ground thyme	⅛ tsp.	0.5 mL
Granulated sugar	1 tsp.	5 mL
Cooked fresh (or cooked frozen, thawed) shelled shrimp	½ lb.	225 g
Cooked white (or brown) rice	2 cups	500 mL

Put first 6 ingredients into 3½ quart (3.5 L) slow cooker. Stir.

Stir bouillon powder into hot water in bowl. Add next 9 ingredients. Stir well. Add to slow cooker. Stir. Cover. Cook on Low for 8 to 9 hours or on High for 4 to 4½ hours.

Add shrimp and rice. Stir. Cover. Cook on High for about 30 minutes until shrimp is heated through. Makes 8 cups (2 L).

1 cup (250 mL): 184 Calories; 1.9 g Total Fat; 695 mg Sodium; 19 g Protein; 22 g Carbohydrate

Paré Pointer

Loaned money may not go as far as it used to, but it is still just as much trouble getting it back.

SHRIMP CREOLE

Lots of good things for color such as green pepper, tomato, mushrooms and shrimp. Serve over rice.

Finely chopped onion	1 cup	250 mL
Chopped celery	½ cup	125 mL
Medium green pepper, chopped	1	1
Canned tomatoes, with juice, broken up	14 oz.	398 mL
Ketchup	2 tbsp.	30 mL
Canned sliced mushrooms, drained	10 oz.	284 mL
Salt	1 tsp.	5 mL
Pepper	¼ tsp.	1 mL
Garlic powder	¼ tsp.	1 mL
Cayenne pepper	¼ tsp.	1 mL
Lemon juice	1 tsp.	5 mL
Parsley flakes	1 tsp.	5 mL
Cooked fresh (or cooked frozen, thawed) shelled shrimp (or 2 cans, 4 oz., 114 g, each, drained)	1 lb.	454 g

Put onion, celery and green pepper into 3½ quart (3.5 L) slow cooker.

Combine next 9 ingredients in bowl. Stir. Pour over top. Cover. Cook on Low for 6 to 8 hours or on High for 3 to 4 hours.

Add shrimp. Stir. Cook on High for 20 to 30 minutes until shrimp is heated through. Stir before serving. Makes 4¼ cups (1 L).

1 cup (250 mL): 165 Calories; 1.7 g Total Fat; 1285 mg Sodium; 25 g Protein; 13 g Carbohydrate; good source of Dietary Fiber

TUNA CASSEROLE

Good combo and a good looking dish.

Chopped onion	½ cup	125 mL
Condensed cream of chicken soup	2 × 10 oz.	2 × 284 mL
Milk	1 cup	250 mL
Frozen peas	10 oz.	300 g
Uncooked medium egg noodles	8 oz.	225 g
Canned flaked tuna, drained	2 × 6½ oz.	2 × 184 g

(continued on next page)

Sprinkle onion in 3½ quart (3.5 L) slow cooker.

Mix soup and milk in large bowl. Add peas, egg noodles and tuna. Stir well. Turn into slow cooker. Smooth top with spoon. Cover. Cook on Low for 5 to 6 hours or on High for 2½ to 3 hours. Stir before serving. Makes 6⅔ cups (1.65 L).

1 cup (250 mL): 329 Calories; 7.5 g Total Fat; 952 mg Sodium; 25 g Protein; 40 g Carbohydrate; good source of Dietary Fiber

SHRIMP MARINARA

Delicious shrimp in an Italian spiced sauce. Serve over rice or pasta.

Canned tomatoes, with juice, broken up	14 oz.	398 mL
Finely chopped onion	1 cup	250 mL
Garlic cloves, minced (or ½ tsp., 2 mL, garlic powder)	2	2
Dried whole oregano	¾ tsp.	4 mL
Salt	1 tsp.	5 mL
Pepper	¼ tsp.	1 mL
Parsley flakes	½ tsp.	2 mL
Granulated sugar	½ tsp.	2 mL
Cooked fresh (or cooked frozen, thawed) shelled shrimp	1 lb.	454 g
Grated Parmesan cheese, sprinkle		

Combine first 8 ingredients in 3½ quart (3.5 L) slow cooker. Cover. Cook on Low for 6 to 7 hours or on High for 3 to 3½ hours until onion is cooked.

Add shrimp. Stir. Cook on High for about 15 minutes until heated through.

Serve over rice or pasta. Sprinkle with cheese. Makes 3⅓ cups (825 mL).

¾ cup (175 mL): 140 Calories; 1.4 g Total Fat; 992 mg Sodium; 23 g Protein; 8 g Carbohydrate

Pictured on page 89.

SEAFOOD CASSEROLE

Mild seafood flavor with a golden cheese topping.

Condensed cream of mushroom soup	10 oz.	284 mL
Water	1 cup	250 mL
Sherry (or alcohol-free sherry)	2 tbsp.	30 mL
Jars of chopped pimiento, drained	2 × 2 oz.	2 × 57 mL
Onion flakes	1 tbsp.	15 mL
Dill weed	½ tsp.	2 mL
Paprika	½ tsp.	2 mL
Parsley flakes	1 tsp.	5 mL
Cayenne pepper	⅛ tsp.	0.5 mL
Canned shrimp, drained	4 oz.	113 g
Canned crabmeat, drained, cartilage removed	4.2 oz.	120 g
Uncooked instant white rice	1½ cups	375 mL
Grated medium Cheddar cheese	1 cup	250 mL

Mix first 9 ingredients in bowl.

Place shrimp, crabmeat and rice in 3½ quart (3.5 L) slow cooker. Pour soup mixture over top. Stir lightly.

Sprinkle with cheese. Cover. Cook on Low for 3 to 4 hours or on High for 1½ to 2 hours. Makes 5 cups (1.25 L).

1 cup (250 mL): 327 Calories; 13.3 g Total Fat; 832 mg Sodium; 18 g Protein; 33 g Carbohydrate

POACHED SALMON

Serve with lemon wedges or tartar sauce.

Salmon fillet	1¼ lbs.	560 g
Chopped chives	1 tsp.	5 mL
Chopped celery	½ cup	125 mL
Small bay leaf	1	1
Onion powder	¼ tsp.	1 mL
Salt	½ tsp.	2 mL
Apple juice (or white wine)	½ cup	125 mL
Water	½ cup	125 mL
Lemon juice	1 tbsp.	15 mL

(continued on next page)

Lay salmon in 3½ quart (3.5 L) slow cooker.

Sprinkle chives, celery and bay leaf beside fillet.

Stir remaining 5 ingredients together in small bowl. Pour over salmon. Cover. Cook on Low for 3 to 4 hours or on High for 2 hours until salmon flakes when tested with fork. Discard bay leaf. Serves 4.

1 serving: *189 Calories; 6.5 g Total Fat; 458 mg Sodium; 28 g Protein; 5 g Carbohydrate*

Pictured on page 71.

POACHED FISH: Substitute your favorite fish in place of salmon.

SALMON PATTIES

Crusty coated patties and condiments make good burgers.

Large eggs, fork-beaten	2	2
Canned salmon, drained, skin and round bones removed	2 × 7.5 oz.	2 × 213 g
Water	½ cup	125 mL
Soda cracker crumbs	1 cup	250 mL
Celery salt	½ tsp.	2 mL
Onion powder	½ tsp.	2 mL
Salt	¼ tsp.	1 mL
Dill weed	¼ tsp.	1 mL
Pepper	$\frac{1}{16}$ tsp.	0.5 mL
Corn flake crumbs	½ cup	125 mL

Combine first 9 ingredients in bowl. Mix well. Shape into 8 patties.

Coat with corn flake crumbs. Place 4 patties in bottom of 3½ quart (3.5 L) or 5 quart (5 L) slow cooker. Place remaining patties on top. Cover. Cook on Low for 4 to 5 hours or on High for 2 to 2½ hours. Makes 4 patties.

1 patty: *171 Calories; 7.7 g Total Fat; 578 mg Sodium; 11 g Protein; 13 g Carbohydrate*

Pictured on page 143.

SALMON LOAF

A very good salmon flavor to this loaf. Dense enough to slice thinly for sandwiches if desired.

Large eggs, fork-beaten	2	2
Reserved liquid from canned salmon		
Lemon juice	1½ tbsp.	25 mL
Onion flakes	1 tbsp.	15 mL
Salt	¾ tsp.	4 mL
Pepper	¼ tsp.	1 mL
Milk	½ cup	125 mL
Fine dry bread crumbs	1½ cups	375 mL
Canned salmon, drained, liquid reserved, skin and round bones removed (red salmon is best for color)	2 × 7.5 oz.	2 × 213 g
CREAM SAUCE		
All-purpose flour	2 tbsp.	30 mL
Parsley flakes	¼ tsp.	1 mL
Salt	½ tsp.	2 mL
Pepper	⅛ tsp.	0.5 mL
Onion powder	¼ tsp.	1 mL
Milk	1 cup	250 mL

Combine eggs, reserved liquid from salmon, lemon juice, onion flakes, salt, pepper and milk in bowl. Stir in bread crumbs.

Flake salmon. Stir into bread crumb mixture. Pack into greased 3½ quart (3.5 L) slow cooker. Pull sides in so it doesn't touch sides of slow cooker. Cover. Cook on Low for 4 to 5 hours or on High for 2 to 2½ hours. Loosen sides with knife. Cuts into 6 wedges. Serve with Cream Sauce.

Cream Sauce: Stir flour, parsley, salt, pepper and onion powder together in saucepan.

Whisk in milk gradually until no lumps remain. Heat and stir until boiling and thickened. Makes 1 cup (250 mL).

1 wedge with 2 tbsp. (30 mL) sauce: 295 Calories; 10.9 g Total Fat; 1125 mg Sodium; 20 g Protein; 28 g Carbohydrate

Pictured on page 35.

A small economical cut of lamb.

Lamb shoulder roast (bone in)	2½ lbs.	1.1 kg
Liquid gravy browner	2 tsp.	10 mL
Salt, sprinkle		
Pepper, sprinkle		

Gravy, page 48

Brush roast with gravy browner. Place in 3½ quart (3.5 L) slow cooker. Sprinkle with salt and pepper. Cover. Cook on Low for 8 to 9 hours or on High for 4 to 4½ hours.

Skim off any fat from remaining juice. Make gravy. Serves 4.

1 serving (with gravy): 331 Calories; 17.6 g Total Fat; 490 mg Sodium; 36 g Protein; 4 g Carbohydrate

LAMB LOAF

A moist firm loaf. Cuts well. Serve very hot or very cold as all lamb should be served.

Large eggs, fork-beaten	2	2
Minced onion	½ cup	125 mL
Beef bouillon powder	2 tsp.	10 mL
Quick-cooking rolled oats (not instant)	1 cup	250 mL
Lean ground lamb	2 lbs.	900 g
Ketchup (optional)	2 tbsp.	30 mL

Combine eggs, onion, bouillon powder and rolled oats in bowl. Stir.

Add ground lamb. Mix. Shape into round loaf and place in 3½ quart (3.5 L) slow cooker, not touching sides.

Spread ketchup over top. Cover. Cook on Low for 7 to 9 hours or on High for 3½ to 4½ hours. Cuts into 8 wedges.

1 wedge: 217 Calories; 7.9 g Total Fat; 239 mg Sodium; 26 g Protein; 8 g Carbohydrate

Paré Pointer

Looking for a job? Try the place with the sign asking for someone to work eight hours a day to replace someone who didn't.

RACK OF LAMB

The coating adds flavor and adds to the appearance. Luscious lamb.

Soda cracker (or fine dry bread) crumbs	1/4 cup	60 mL
Dried rosemary, crushed	1/4 tsp.	1 mL
Ground thyme	1/4 tsp.	1 mL
Dried mint (optional)	1/4 tsp.	1 mL
Garlic powder	1/4 tsp.	1 mL
Parsley flakes	2 tsp.	10 mL
Salt	1/4 tsp.	1 mL
Pepper	1/4 tsp.	1 mL
Rack of lamb (or shoulder roast)	3 3/4 lbs.	1.7 kg
Cooking oil	1 tsp.	5 mL

Gravy, page 48

Combine first 8 ingredients in bowl. Mix well.

Rub rounded fat side of roast with cooking oil. Sprinkle with dry mixture. Press dry mixture against roast. Place in 5 quart (5 L) slow cooker, thin end at top. Cover. Cook on Low for 10 to 11 hours or on High for 5 to 5 1/2 hours. Temperature should be 180°F (82°C) for well done.

Skim off any fat from remaining juice. Make gravy. Serves 4.

1 serving (with gravy): 502 Calories; 27.6 g Total Fat; 647 mg Sodium; 54 g Protein; 6 g Carbohydrate

1. Carrot Cake, page 66
2. Roast Chicken, page 115
3. Cranberry Sauce, page 128
4. Shrimp Marinara, page 83
5. Easy Bean Soup, page 138
6. Tomato Herb Bread, page 59

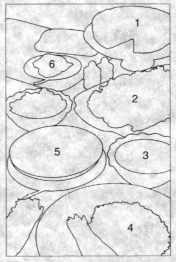

Props Courtesy Of: Creations By Design; Eaton's; Stokes; The Bay

Easy and quick to prepare. Looks great.

Pork loin chops, trimmed of fat	6	6
Liquid gravy browner	1 tsp.	5 mL
Condensed chicken and rice soup	10 oz.	284 mL

Brush both sides of pork chops with gravy browner. Place in 3½ quart (3.5 L) slow cooker.

Pour soup over top. Spread evenly. Cover. Cook on Low for 9 to 10 hours or on High for 4½ to 5 hours. Serves 6.

1 serving: 169 Calories; 6.5 g Total Fat; 417 mg Sodium; 23 g Protein; 3 g Carbohydrate

Good sauce, just asking to be spooned over rice. Even good on potatoes or noodles.

Lean pork, cubed	2¼ lbs.	1 kg
Brown sugar, packed	1 cup	250 mL
Water	1 cup	250 mL
White vinegar	½ cup	125 mL
Soy sauce	1 tbsp.	15 mL
Water	⅓ cup	75 mL
Cornstarch	¼ cup	60 mL

Place pork in 3½ quart (3.5 L) slow cooker.

Mix brown sugar and first amount of water in bowl. Add vinegar and soy sauce. Stir. Pour over pork. Cover. Cook on Low for 8 to 10 hours or on High for 4 to 5 hours. Tilt slow cooker and skim off any fat.

Stir second amount of water and cornstarch together in bowl. Add to slow cooker. Cook on High for 15 to 20 minutes to thicken or pour into large saucepan to thicken on burner. Serves 6 to 8.

⅙ recipe: 304 Calories; 3.9 g Total Fat; 240 mg Sodium; 23 g Protein; 44 g Carbohydrate

Paré Pointer

Love and concern for one another don't make the world go round, but they make the ride worth it all.

PORK LOIN ROAST

Serve slices of pork with this exquisite sauce and make gravy for potatoes from leftover juice. Sauce can be made ahead and reheated.

Boneless pork roast	3 lbs.	1.4 kg
Salt, sprinkle (optional)		
Pepper, sprinkle (optional)		
SPICY CRANBERRY SAUCE		
Granulated sugar	½ cup	125 mL
Cornstarch	2 tbsp.	30 mL
Dry mustard	1 tsp.	5 mL
Ground cloves	¼ tsp.	1 mL
Cranberry cocktail	2 cups	500 mL
Gravy, page 48 (optional)		

Place roast in 3½ quart (3.5 L) slow cooker. Sprinkle with salt and pepper. Cover. Cook on Low for 8 to 10 hours or on High for 4 to 5 hours. Serves 6.

Spicy Cranberry Sauce: Measure first 4 ingredients into saucepan. Mix well.

Add cranberry cocktail. Heat and stir until boiling and thickened. Serve with pork. Makes 2 cups (500 mL).

Make gravy with remaining juice from roast to serve over potatoes if desired. Serves 6 to 8.

⅙ recipe: 347 Calories; 8.7 g Total Fat; 96 mg Sodium; 32 g Protein; 33 g Carbohydrate

Paré Pointer

Monsters will only drink ghoul-ade.

STUFFED PORK ROAST

A neat looking slice with a dark slice of prune in center of light-colored meat.

Dried pitted prunes, approximately	**6-8**	**6-8**
Boneless pork loins, tied together	**2**	**2**
(about 3 lbs., 1.4 kg)		
Liquid gravy browner	**2 tsp.**	**10 mL**
Gravy, page 48		

Push prunes down in between tied pork loins.

Brush roast with gravy browner. Place in 3½ quart (3.5 L) or 5 quart (5 L) slow cooker. Cover. Cook on Low for 8 to 10 hours or on High for 4 to 5 hours.

Make gravy with remaining juice from pork. Serves 6 to 8.

⅙ recipe: 641 Calories; 46.8 g Total Fat; 400 mg Sodium; 44 g Protein; 8 g Carbohydrate

Pictured on page 17.

PORK AND CABBAGE

With apple included, this is not only flavorful but an interesting dish.

Coarsely chopped cabbage (about	**1¼ lbs.**	**560 g**
5 cups, 1.25 L)		
Sliced onion	**1 cup**	**250 mL**
Salt, sprinkle		
Pepper, sprinkle		
Medium cooking apples (such as	**2**	**2**
McIntosh), peeled, cored and sliced		
Granulated sugar	**2 tbsp.**	**30 mL**
Boneless lean pork shoulder, cubed	**1½ lbs.**	**680 g**

Layer first 6 ingredients in 3½ quart (3.5 L) slow cooker.

Place cubed pork on top. Cover. Cook on Low for 9 to 10 hours or on High for 4½ to 5 hours. Makes 6⅓ cups (1.6 L).

1 cup (250 mL): 213 Calories; 6 g Total Fat; 98 mg Sodium; 23 g Protein; 16 g Carbohydrate

CHERRY PORK CHOPS

Mildly spiced pie filling cooks with pork chops, giving them a different flavor and adding color.

Pork loin chops, trimmed of fat	6	6
Liquid gravy browner	1 tsp.	5 mL
Salt, sprinkle		
Pepper, sprinkle		
Cherry pie filling	$\frac{1}{2}$ × 19 oz.	$\frac{1}{2}$ × 540 mL
Cider vinegar	1$\frac{1}{2}$ tsp.	7 mL
Prepared mustard	1 tsp.	5 mL
Ground cloves	$\frac{1}{16}$ tsp.	0.5 mL

Brush both sides of pork chops with gravy browner. Sprinkle with salt and pepper.

Stir pie filling, vinegar, mustard and cloves together in bowl. Layer pork chops with cherry sauce in 5 quart (5 L) slow cooker. Cover. Cook on Low for 9 to 10 hours or on High for 4$\frac{1}{2}$ to 5 hours. Spoon juice over pork chops. Serves 6.

1 serving: 202 Calories; 5.9 g Total Fat; 102 mg Sodium; 22 g Protein; 15 g Carbohydrate

Pictured on page 107.

PORK CHOP CASSEROLE

Lots of onion rings over the chops. Ends up with some good gravy.

Pork loin chops, trimmed of fat	6	6
Liquid gravy browner	1 tsp.	5 mL
Medium onion, thinly sliced, separated into rings	1	1
Condensed cream of potato soup	10 oz.	284 mL
Non-fat sour cream	1 cup	250 mL
Ground thyme	$\frac{1}{4}$ tsp.	1 mL

Brush both sides of pork chops with gravy browner. Place in 3$\frac{1}{2}$ quart (3.5 L) slow cooker.

Scatter onion rings over top.

Mix soup, sour cream and thyme in bowl. Spoon over top. Cover. Cook on Low for 9 to 10 hours or on High for 4$\frac{1}{2}$ to 5 hours. Serves 6.

1 serving: 192 Calories; 6.7 g Total Fat; 508 mg Sodium; 24 g Protein; 8 g Carbohydrate

BARBECUE PORK BUNS

Serve pork mixture in buns, or serve open-faced. Dark red sauce.

Lean pork roast, cubed	2 lbs.	900 g
Tomato sauce	7.5 oz.	213 mL
Ketchup	½ cup	125 mL
Chopped onion	1 cup	250 mL
White vinegar	⅓ cup	75 mL
Brown sugar, packed	⅓ cup	75 mL
Prepared mustard	1 tsp.	5 mL
Worcestershire sauce	1 tsp.	5 mL
Chili powder	1 tsp.	5 mL
Salt	¼ tsp.	1 mL
Molasses (not blackstrap)	2 tbsp.	30 mL
Water	⅔ cup	150 mL
Hamburger buns, split (buttered, optional)	8	8

Combine first 12 ingredients in 3½ quart (3.5 L) slow cooker. Cover. Cook on Low for 8 to 10 hours or on High for 4 to 5 hours.

Remove pork with slotted spoon to large bowl. Working with a few pieces at a time on plate, shred pork with 2 forks. Pork may be stirred into sauce and served over each bun half, or may be inserted into buns as a sandwich. Makes 16 open-faced buns or 8 sandwich buns.

1 open-faced bun (with sauce): 238 Calories; 7.9 g Total Fat; 397 mg Sodium; 18 g Protein; 23 g Carbohydrate

More and more electricians are driving Voltz Wagons.

PORK CHOPS

Colorful with tomato and french-cut green beans.

Canned tomatoes, with juice, cut up	14 oz.	398 mL
Canned french-cut green beans, drained	2 × 14 oz.	2 × 398 mL
Chopped onion	1 cup	250 mL
Garlic powder (or 1 clove, minced)	¼ tsp.	1 mL
Granulated sugar	1 tsp.	5 mL
Pork chops, trimmed of fat	6	6
Liquid gravy browner	1 tsp.	5 mL

Place first 5 ingredients in 5 quart (5 L) slow cooker. Stir.

Brush both sides of pork chops with gravy browner. Layer over vegetables. Cover. Cook on Low for 10 to 12 hours or on High for 5 to 6 hours. Remove pork chops to platter. Use slotted spoon to remove vegetables or serve in sauce as is. Serves 6.

1 serving: 182 Calories; 5.9 g Total Fat; 318 mg Sodium; 23 g Protein; 9 g Carbohydrate

PORK CHOP DINNER

A complete dinner. A good mushroom gravy to serve over the pork chops.

Small bite-size pieces of carrot	1½ cups	375 mL
Small bite-size pieces of potato	2½ cups	625 mL
Small bite-size pieces of onion	1 cup	250 mL
Small bite-size pieces of parsnip	1 cup	250 mL
Pork loin chops, trimmed of fat	6	6
Liquid gravy browner	1 tsp.	5 mL
Condensed cream of mushroom soup	10 oz.	284 mL
Water	½ cup	125 mL

Put carrot in 5 quart (5 L) slow cooker. Layer potato, onion and parsnip over top.

Brush both sides of pork chops with gravy browner. Lay over parsnip.

Stir soup and water together in bowl. Pour over all. Cover. Cook on Low for 9 to 10 hours or on High for 4½ to 5 hours. Serves 6.

1 serving: 291 Calories; 9.8 g Total Fat; 516 mg Sodium; 25 g Protein; 26 g Carbohydrate; good source of Dietary Fiber

SPICY PORK CHOPS

An excellent spicy sauce on these browned pork chops.

Pork loin chops, trimmed of fat	6	6
Liquid gravy browner	1 tsp.	5 mL
Ketchup	⅓ cup	75 mL
White vinegar	⅓ cup	75 mL
Water	⅔ cup	150 mL
Celery salt	1 tsp.	5 mL
Prepared mustard	1 tsp.	5 mL
Ground cloves	½ tsp.	2 mL
Granulated sugar	1 tsp.	5 mL

Brush both sides of pork chops with gravy browner. Arrange in 3½ quart (3.5 L) slow cooker.

Mix remaining 7 ingredients in bowl. Pour over pork chops, lifting pork chops to get a bit in between. Cover. Cook on Low for 9 to 10 hours or on High for 4½ to 5 hours. Serves 6.

1 serving: 168 Calories; 5.9 g Total Fat; 518 mg Sodium; 22 g Protein; 6 g Carbohydrate

PORK AND APPLES

Apples are a natural go-with. They taste great and aren't sweet when cooked. Some clear juice to pour over pork chops.

Pork loin chops, trimmed of fat, about 1 inch (2.5 cm) thick	4	4
Liquid gravy browner	1 tsp.	5 mL
Salt, sprinkle		
Pepper, sprinkle		
Medium cooking apples (such as McIntosh), peeled, cored and sliced	2	2
Granulated sugar	½ tsp.	2 mL

Brush both sides of pork chops with gravy browner. Arrange pork chops in 4½ quart (4.5 L) slow cooker. If cooker isn't big enough to hold in 1 layer, make 2 layers. Sprinkle with salt and pepper. Cover with apple slices.

Sprinkle with sugar. Cover. Cook on Low for 8 to 10 hours or on High for 4 to 5 hours. Serves 4.

1 serving: 185 Calories; 5.9 g Total Fat; 104 mg Sodium; 22 g Protein; 11 g Carbohydrate

STUFFED PORK CHOPS

Chops aren't served this way very often. Easy to prepare. A definite company dish.

STUFFING

Fine dry bread crumbs	$7/8$ cup	200 mL
Finely chopped celery	1 tbsp.	15 mL
Finely chopped onion	$1/4$ cup	60 mL
Poultry seasoning	$1/4$ tsp.	1 mL
Parsley flakes	$1/4$ tsp.	1 mL
Salt	$1/4$ tsp.	1 mL
Pepper	$1/16$ tsp.	0.5 mL
Hot water	$2/3$ cup	150 mL
Chicken bouillon powder	$1/2$ tsp.	2 mL
Thick lean pork chops, slit horizontally to make pockets (see Note)	6	6

Stuffing: Mix first 7 ingredients in bowl.

Stir hot water and bouillon powder together in small cup. Pour over stuffing mixture. Toss, adding more water if needed to moisten.

Stuff pockets in pork chops. Arrange in slow cooker. Cover. Cook on Low for 8 to 10 hours or on High for 4 to 5 hours. Serves 6.

Note: Either you or your butcher can slit sides of chops to make pockets.

1 serving: 283 Calories; 9.3 g Total Fat; 383 mg Sodium; 34 g Protein; 13 g Carbohydrate

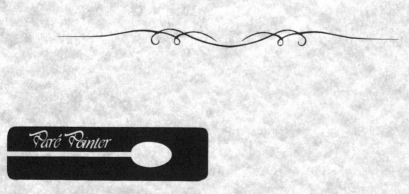

Most hairdressers take a short cut to their barbershops.

SWEET AND SOUR RIBS

Superb! Glazed well and delicious.

BROWN SUGAR SAUCE

Brown sugar, packed	2 cups	500 mL
All-purpose flour	¼ cup	60 mL
Water	⅓ cup	75 mL
White vinegar	½ cup	125 mL
Soy sauce	2 tbsp.	30 mL
Ketchup	2 tbsp.	30 mL
Ground ginger	¼ tsp.	1 mL
Garlic powder	¼ tsp.	1 mL
Meaty pork spareribs, cut into 2 or 3 rib sections	3 lbs.	1.4 kg

Brown Sugar Sauce: Mix brown sugar and flour in saucepan. Add water. Stir. Add next 5 ingredients. Heat and stir until boiling and thickened.

Layer ribs in a 5 quart (5 L) slow cooker, spooning sauce over each layer. Cover. Cook on Low for 10 to 12 hours or on High for 5 to 6 hours until ribs are very tender. Serves 6.

1 serving: 598 Calories; 20.8 g Total Fat; 516 mg Sodium; 22 g Protein; 82 g Carbohydrate

BARBECUED SPARERIBS

Reddish-brown ribs with a smoky barbecue flavor. Lots of sauce to spoon over rice, noodles or potatoes.

Meaty pork spareribs, cut into 2 or 3 rib sections	3 lbs.	1.4 kg
Chopped or sliced onion	1½ cups	375 mL
Smoky barbecue sauce	2 cups	500 mL

Place ½ of ribs in 3½ quart (3.5 L) slow cooker. Sprinkle ½ of onion over top. Spoon ½ of barbecue sauce over onion. Repeat layers with second ½ of ribs, onion and barbecue sauce. Cover. Cook on Low for 10 to 12 hours or on High for 5 to 6 hours. Serves 6.

1 serving: 358 Calories; 22.4 g Total Fat; 795 mg Sodium; 23 g Protein; 15 g Carbohydrate; excellent source of Dietary Fiber

POLYNESIAN RIBS

Sauce has a wonderful pineapple flavor. Lots of juice to use as gravy.

Brown sugar, packed	¼ cup	60 mL
All-purpose flour	⅓ cup	75 mL
White vinegar	¼ cup	60 mL
Ketchup	¼ cup	60 mL
Canned crushed pineapple, with juice	14 oz.	398 mL
Soy sauce	1 tbsp.	15 mL
Salt	½ tsp.	2 mL
Pepper	⅛ tsp.	0.5 mL
Pork spareribs, cut into 2 rib sections	3 lbs.	1.4 kg

Measure first 8 ingredients into saucepan. Heat and stir until boiling and thickened. Pour ⅓ of sauce into slow cooker.

Arrange ½ of ribs over top. Cover with second ⅓ of sauce followed by second ½ of ribs. Cover with remaining ⅓ of sauce. Cover. Cook on Low for 10 to 12 hours or on High for 5 to 6 hours. Serves 6.

1 serving: 397 Calories; 20.9 g Total Fat; 624 mg Sodium; 22 g Protein; 30 g Carbohydrate

RIBS 'N' STUFFING

Yummy ribs with stuffing as a bonus.

Box of stuffing mix, with seasoning	4½ oz.	120 g
Meaty pork spareribs, cut into 2 or 3 rib sections	3 lbs.	1.4 kg

Prepare stuffing according to package directions.

Place ribs in 6 quart (6 L) slow cooker. Ribs can be placed on trivet to allow fat to run to bottom if desired. Wrap prepared stuffing in foil leaving top partially open. Set on top of ribs. Cover. Cook on Low for 9 to 10 hours or on High for 4½ to 5 hours. Serves 6.

1 serving: 385 Calories; 25.4 g Total Fat; 388 mg Sodium; 23 g Protein; 15 g Carbohydrate

Paré Pointer

Mother worm to little worm, "Where in earth have you been?"

So easy to do; you end up with nicely browned ribs.

Meaty pork spareribs, cut into **2 or 3 rib sections**	**3 lbs.**	**1.4 kg**
Liquid gravy browner	**2 tsp.**	**10 mL**

Brush ribs with gravy browner. Put into 3½ quart (3.5 L) slow cooker. Cover. Cook on Low for 9 to 10 hours or on High for 4½ to 5 hours. Serves 6.

1 serving: 280 Calories; 20.8 g Total Fat; 133 mg Sodium; 21 g Protein; 1 g Carbohydrate

A good combination to cook together. Tasty.

Chopped or sliced onion	**1 cup**	**250 mL**
Large cooking apple (such as **McIntosh), peeled, cored and sliced**	**1**	**1**
Canned sauerkraut, drained	**14 oz.**	**398 mL**
Meaty pork spareribs, cut into **2 or 3 rib sections**	**3 lbs.**	**1.4 kg**
Salt, sprinkle		
Pepper, sprinkle		
Dill weed	**1 tsp.**	**5 mL**
Water	**½ cup**	**125 mL**

Put onion into 5 quart (5 L) slow cooker. Lay apple slices over top. Spoon sauerkraut over apple.

Sprinkle ribs with salt and pepper. Place over sauerkraut.

Combine dill weed and water in small cup. Stir. Pour over all. Cover. Cook on Low for 10 to 12 hours or on High for 5 to 6 hours. Serves 6.

1 serving: 312 Calories; 20.9 g Total Fat; 515 mg Sodium; 22 g Protein; 9 g Carbohydrate

Paré Pointer

Never lend money to a football player. Sometimes you get a quarterback and if you're lucky, a halfback.

GLAZED HAM

Such an easy way to cook a ham. Glaze is very tasty.

Boneless ham, trimmed of fat	**5 lbs.**	**2.3 kg**
Orange marmalade	**¼ cup**	**60 mL**
Prepared mustard	**1 tbsp.**	**15 mL**
Prepared horseradish	**½ tsp.**	**2 mL**
Ground cloves	**¹⁄₁₆ tsp.**	**0.5 mL**

Gravy, page 48

Place ham in 6 quart (6 L) slow cooker. Cut ham in half, if necessary, to fit in slow cooker.

Combine marmalade, mustard, horseradish and cloves in small bowl. Stir. Spread over ham. Cover. Cook on Low for 8 to 9 hours or on High for 4 to 4½ hours.

Make gravy with remaining liquid. Serves 12.

1 serving: 273 Calories; 9.5 g Total Fat; 2827 mg Sodium; 37 g Protein; 8 g Carbohydrate

Pictured on page 71.

SCALLOPED HAM MEAL

Vegetables and ham cook while you do something else.

Medium potatoes, sliced ¼ inch (6 mm) thick	**4**	**4**
Chopped onion	**1 cup**	**250 mL**
Salt, sprinkle		
Pepper, sprinkle		
Frozen peas	**2 cups**	**500 mL**
Smoked ham (or smoked pork shoulder piece), sliced ½ inch (12 mm) thick	**2 lbs.**	**900 g**
Condensed cream of chicken soup	**10 oz.**	**284 mL**
Water	**1 cup**	**250 mL**

Put potato into 3½ quart (3.5 L) slow cooker. Scatter onion over top. Sprinkle with salt and pepper. Sprinkle with peas. Lay ham slices on top.

Stir soup and water together in bowl. Pour over ham. Cover. Cook on Low for 9 to 10 hours or on High for 4½ to 5 hours. Serves 6.

1 serving: 352 Calories; 10.7 g Total Fat; 2600 mg Sodium; 35 g Protein; 28 g Carbohydrate; good source of Dietary Fiber

Pictured on page 143.

HAM STEAKS

Pineapple slices and cranberries make these very showy and flavorful.

Ham steak (about 1 inch, 2.5 cm, thick)	1½ lbs.	680 g
Pineapple slices	6	6
Brown sugar, packed	⅓ cup	75 mL
Fresh (or frozen) cranberries	¼ cup	60 mL
Ground cloves	⅛ tsp.	0.5 mL
Prepared orange juice	⅓ cup	75 mL

Place ham in 5 quart (5 L) slow cooker. Lay pineapple slices over top.

Mash brown sugar and cranberries together in small bowl. Add cloves and orange juice. Mix. Pour over pineapple. Cover. Cook on Low for 8 to 10 hours or on High for 4 to 5 hours. Cut ham into serving-size pieces. Serves 4.

1 serving: 320 Calories; 7.3 g Total Fat; 2164 mg Sodium; 34 g Protein; 29 g Carbohydrate

Pictured on page 53.

HAM LOAF

Use your leftover ham for this loaf. Easy to double recipe. Very tasty.

Ground ham	3 cups	750 mL
Quick-cooking rolled oats (not instant)	¾ cup	175 mL
Milk	¼ cup	60 mL
Large eggs	2	2
Prepared mustard	1 tbsp.	15 mL
Minced onion	2 tbsp.	30 mL
TOPPING		
Brown sugar, packed	⅓ cup	75 mL
Prepared mustard	2 tsp.	10 mL
Prepared orange juice	1 tbsp.	15 mL

Place first 6 ingredients in bowl. Mix well. Pack in 3½ quart (3.5 L) slow cooker.

Topping: Combine brown sugar, mustard and orange juice in small cup. Stir. Spread over loaf. Cover. Cook on Low for 6 to 7 hours or on High for 3 to 3½ hours. Serves 4.

1 serving: 302 Calories; 8.4 g Total Fat; 1395 mg Sodium; 24 g Protein; 33 g Carbohydrate

HAM POTATO BAKE

Color is fantastic with sweet potato and ham. A festive taste to be sure.

Small sweet potatoes, peeled, cut into bite-size pieces	2½ lbs.	1.1 kg
Boneless ham steak	1½ lbs.	680 g
Brown sugar, packed	⅓ cup	75 mL
Prepared mustard	1 tsp.	5 mL

Put sweet potato into 3½ quart (3.5 L) slow cooker. Place ham steak over top.

Mix brown sugar and mustard in small cup. Sprinkle over ham. Cover. Cook on Low for 7 to 8 hours or on High for 3½ to 4 hours. Cut ham into serving-size pieces. Serves 4.

1 serving: 580 Calories; 8.3 g Total Fat; 2250 mg Sodium; 38 g Protein; 88 g Carbohydrate; excellent source of Dietary Fiber

HAM AND NOODLES

In a delicious Parmesan cheese sauce with mushrooms.

Cubed cooked ham	1½ cups	375 mL
Canned whole or sliced mushrooms, drained	10 oz.	284 mL
Condensed cream of mushroom soup	10 oz.	284 mL
Water	½ cup	125 mL
Prepared horseradish	1½ tsp.	7 mL
Grated Parmesan cheese	¼ cup	60 mL
Sherry (or alcohol-free sherry)	2 tbsp.	30 mL
Uncooked broad egg noodles	2 cups	500 mL
Water	1 cup	250 mL

Place ham cubes and mushrooms in 3½ quart (3.5 L) slow cooker.

Combine soup and first amount of water in bowl. Add horseradish, cheese and sherry. Stir. Add to slow cooker. Cover. Cook on Low for 6 to 8 hours or on High for 3 to 4 hours.

Add noodles and second amount of water. Stir. Cover. Cook on High for 15 to 20 minutes until noodles are tender. Makes scant 4 cups (1 L).

1 cup (250 mL): 273 Calories; 11.5 g Total Fat; 1701 mg Sodium; 18 g Protein; 23 g Carbohydrate

HASH BROWN CASSEROLE

Oniony, cheesy and yummy.

Condensed cream of mushroom soup	10 oz.	284 mL
Finely chopped onion	½ cup	125 mL
Non-fat sour cream	1 cup	250 mL
Salt	1 tsp.	5 mL
Pepper	¼ tsp.	1 mL
Frozen hash brown potatoes	2¼ lbs.	1 kg
Grated sharp Cheddar cheese	1 cup	250 mL
TOPPING		
Hard margarine (or butter)	1 tbsp.	15 mL
Corn flake crumbs	¼ cup	60 mL

Stir first 5 ingredients in large bowl.

Add potato and cheese. Turn into slow cooker. Cover. Cook on High for 3 to 4 hours.

Topping: Melt margarine in small saucepan. Stir in corn flake crumbs. Sauté until crisp. Scatter over top before serving. Makes 6 cups (1.5 L).

⅔ cup (150 mL): 212 Calories; 9 g Total Fat; 734 mg Sodium; 7 g Protein; 27 g Carbohydrate

JACKET POTATOES

Potatoes may be wrapped in foil, left dry or the skin greased. They all cook in the same time. Serve with sour cream, bacon bits and chives.

Medium baking potatoes, with peel	6	6

Poke potatoes with sharp knife. Wrap with foil if desired. Arrange, ends down, in a 5 quart (5 L) slow cooker. Cover. Cook on Low for 8 to 10 hours. Makes 6 potatoes.

1 potato: 111 Calories; 0.2 g Total Fat; 11 mg Sodium; 3 g Protein; 25 g Carbohydrate

Paré Pointer

Never play chess outside. Haven't you heard that squirrels eat chess-nuts?

SCALLOPED HAM POTATOES

Creamy sauce over vegetables and ham. Cheese adds extra flavor.

Water	1 cup	250 mL
Cream of tartar	½ tsp.	2 mL
Medium potatoes, thinly sliced	5	5
Chopped onion	1 cup	250 mL
Salt, sprinkle		
Pepper, sprinkle		
SAUCE		
All-purpose flour	¼ cup	60 mL
Salt	1 tsp.	5 mL
Pepper	⅛ tsp.	0.5 mL
Milk	2 cups	500 mL
Grated medium or sharp Cheddar cheese (optional)	1 cup	250 mL
Cubed boneless smoked ham	2 cups	500 mL

Combine water and cream of tartar in large bowl. Stir. Add potato. Stir well. This will help keep potato from darkening. Drain. Layer potato and onion in 5 quart (5 L) slow cooker. Sprinkle with salt and pepper.

Sauce: Stir flour, salt and pepper together in saucepan. Whisk in milk gradually until no lumps remain. Heat and stir until boiling. Pour ½ of sauce over vegetables.

Sprinkle with cheese and ham. Cover with remaining ½ of sauce. Cover. Cook on Low for 9 to 10 hours or on High for 4½ to 5 hours. Serves 6.

1 serving: 207 Calories; 3.6 g Total Fat; 1239 mg Sodium; 15 g Protein; 28 g Carbohydrate

1. Cherry Pork Chops, page 94
2. Lemonade Chicken, page 123
3. Sufferin' Succotash, page 23
4. Marbled Cheesecake, page 80
5. Spicy Spaghetti Sauce, page 28
6. Acorn Squash, page 149

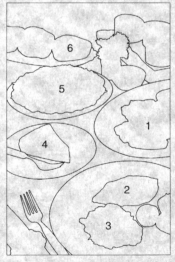

Props Courtesy Of: Eaton's; La Cache; Le Gnome; Stokes; The Bay; The Glasshouse; The Royal Doulton Store

Arrive home to hot baked potatoes. Prepare stuffing while oven heats.

Medium baking potatoes	6	6
Water	2 tbsp.	30 mL
STUFFING		
Light cream cheese, softened	4 oz.	125 g
Non-fat sour cream	⅔ cup	150 mL
Onion salt	1½ tsp.	7 mL
Chopped chives	1 tbsp.	15 mL
Salt	½ tsp.	2 mL
Pepper	⅛ tsp.	0.5 mL
Grated medium Cheddar cheese	⅓ cup	75 mL
Paprika, sprinkle		

Arrange potato in 3½ quart (3.5 L) slow cooker, stacking if necessary. Add water. Cover. Cook on Low for 8 to 10 hours.

Stuffing: Mash first 6 ingredients together in bowl. Cut lengthwise slice from top of each potato. Scoop hot potato into same bowl leaving shells intact. Mash well. Spoon back into shells.

Sprinkle with cheese and paprika. Arrange in single layer in 9 x 13 inch (22 x 33 cm) baking pan. Bake in 425°F (220°C) oven for about 15 minutes until hot. Makes 6 stuffed potatoes.

1 stuffed potato: 188 Calories; 5.8 g Total Fat; 827 mg Sodium; 8 g Protein; 27 g Carbohydrate

Pictured on page 125.

Little Mary thinks children grow in a kindergarden.

SCALLOPED POTATOES

A breeze to make. Creamy good.

Water	2 cups	500 mL
Cream of tartar	1 tsp.	5 mL
Medium potatoes, quartered lengthwise and thinly sliced	5	5
All-purpose flour	¼ cup	60 mL
Salt	1 tsp.	5 mL
Pepper	⅛ tsp.	0.5 mL
Milk	1½ cups	375 mL
Grated sharp Cheddar cheese	½ cup	125 mL

Combine water and cream of tartar in large bowl. Stir.

Add potato. Stir well. This will help keep potatoes from darkening. Drain. Turn potato into 4 quart (4 L) slow cooker.

Stir flour, salt and pepper together in saucepan.

Whisk in milk gradually until no lumps remain. Heat and stir until boiling and thickened.

Stir in cheese to melt. Pour over potato. Cover. Cook on Low for 6 to 8 hours. Makes 4 cups (1 L).

⅔ cup (150 mL): 161 Calories; 4.1 g Total Fat; 552 mg Sodium; 7 g Protein; 24 g Carbohydrate

Pictured on page 35.

STUFFED SWEET POTATOES

Delicious. Pineapple flavor comes through with pecans giving a nice crunch.

Medium sweet potatoes (or yams)	6	6
Canned crushed pineapple, with juice	1 cup	250 mL
Grated medium Cheddar cheese	¼ cup	60 mL
Hard margarine (or butter), melted	1 tbsp.	15 mL
Salt	¾ tsp.	4 mL
Pepper	⅛ tsp.	0.5 mL
Finely chopped pecans	2 tbsp.	30 mL
Paprika, sprinkle		

(continued on next page)

Place sweet potato, pointed ends up, in a 5 quart (5 L) slow cooker Cover. Cook on Low for 7 to 8 hours. Cut thick slice from top lengthwise. Scoop out pulp into bowl, leaving shell 1/4 inch (6 mm) thick.

Add next 5 ingredients to potato pulp. Mash well. Spoon back into shells.

Sprinkle with pecans and paprika. Arrange on baking pan. Bake in 425°F (220°C) oven for 15 to 20 minutes until hot. Serves 6.

1 stuffed potato: 216 Calories; 5.6 g Total Fat; 409 mg Sodium; 4 g Protein; 39 g Carbohydrate; good source of Dietary Fiber

BEEFY MACARONI

One of the best looking casseroles from a slow cooker. Tastes great too!

Finely chopped onion	1 cup	250 mL
Uncooked elbow macaroni	2 cups	500 mL
Lean ground beef	1 1/2 lbs.	680 g
All-purpose flour	1/4 cup	60 mL
Salt	1 tsp.	5 mL
Pepper	1/4 tsp.	1 mL
Milk	3 cups	750 mL
Canned sliced mushrooms, drained	10 oz.	284 mL
Frozen peas, thawed (2 1/4 cups, 560 mL)	10 oz.	300 g

Place onion and macaroni in 3 1/2 quart (3.5 L) slow cooker.

Scramble-fry ground beef in non-stick frying pan until no longer pink. Drain. Add to slow cooker.

Stir flour, salt and pepper together in small saucepan. Whisk in milk gradually until no lumps remain. Heat, stirring constantly, until boiling and thickened. Pour over ground beef in slow cooker. Stir.

Sprinkle mushrooms and peas over top. Cover. Cook on Low for 3 to 4 hours or on High for 1 1/2 to 2 hours. Makes 8 1/2 cups (2.1 L).

1 cup (250 mL): 309 Calories; 8.3 g Total Fat; 507 mg Sodium; 23 g Protein; 34 g Carbohydrate; good source of Dietary Fiber

Paré Pointer

Little Johnny knows how to make an egg roll. Just push it.

MACARONI AND CHEESE

A simple one pot meal everyone will enjoy.

All-purpose flour	1/4 cup	60 mL
Salt	1 tsp.	5 mL
Pepper	1/4 tsp.	1 mL
Minced onion flakes	2 tbsp.	30 mL
Paprika	1/2 tsp.	2 mL
Milk	3 cups	750 mL
Grated medium or sharp Cheddar cheese	1 cup	250 mL
Uncooked elbow macaroni	2 cups	500 mL

Stir first 5 ingredients in saucepan.

Whisk in milk gradually until no lumps remain. Heat and stir until boiling and thickened.

Add cheese and macaroni. Stir. Turn into 3½ quart (3.5 L) slow cooker. Cover. Cook on Low for 2 to 2½ hours or on High for about 1 hour. Makes 4 cups (1 L).

1 cup (250 mL): 449 Calories; 13 g Total Fat; 965 mg Sodium; 22 g Protein; 60 g Carbohydrate

CHILI PASTA BAKE

Reddish color and a great taste.

Lean ground beef	1½ lbs.	680 g
Chopped onion	1 cup	250 mL
Canned tomatoes, with juice, mashed	2 × 14 oz.	2 × 398 mL
Chili powder	2 tsp.	10 mL
Dried whole oregano	1/2 tsp.	2 mL
Tomato sauce	7.5 oz.	213 mL
Salt	1 tsp.	5 mL
Pepper	1/4 tsp.	1 mL
Uncooked elbow macaroni	1¼ cups	300 mL
Grated Monterey Jack (or medium Cheddar) cheese	1 cup	250 mL

(continued on next page)

Scramble-fry ground beef in non-stick frying pan until browned. Drain well. Transfer to 3½ quart (3.5 L) slow cooker.

Add next 8 ingredients. Stir. Cover. Cook on Low for 5 to 7 hours or on High for 2½ to 3½ hours.

Sprinkle cheese over top. Cook on High for 10 to 15 minutes until cheese is melted. Makes 7 cups (1.75 L).

1 cup (250 mL): 329 Calories; 14 g Total Fat; 904 mg Sodium; 26 g Protein; 25 g Carbohydrate

BEEF AND PASTA

Large shaped pasta adds visual texture to this. Good flavor.

Canned tomatoes, with juice, broken up	2 × 14 oz.	2 × 398 mL
Water	1½ cups	375 mL
Parsley flakes	1 tsp.	5 mL
Garlic powder	¼ tsp.	1 mL
Onion powder	¼ tsp.	1 mL
Salt	1 tsp.	5 mL
Pepper	¼ tsp.	1 mL
Liquid gravy browner	1 tsp.	5 mL
Lean ground beef	1½ lbs.	680 g
Rotini pasta (scant 4 cups, 1 L)	8 oz.	250 g

Combine first 8 ingredients in large bowl. Stir well.

Add ground beef. Mix. Turn into 3½ quart (3.5 L) slow cooker. Cover. Cook on Low for 6 to 8 hours or on High for 3 to 4 hours.

Add pasta. Stir. Cook on High for 15 to 20 minutes until tender. Makes 8 cups (2 L).

1 cup (250 mL): 322 Calories; 13.6 g Total Fat; 584 mg Sodium; 21 g Protein; 28 g Carbohydrate

Paré Pointer

No one will ever steal this clock. The employees always watch it.

CHICKEN À LA KING

Good, mild and flavorful. Green pepper and pimiento add color. Serve in pastry cups for a company event.

Finely chopped celery	¼ cup	60 mL
Chopped onion	½ cup	125 mL
Medium green pepper, diced	1	1
Small fresh mushrooms, sliced	3 cups	750 mL
Jar of chopped pimiento, drained	2 oz.	57 mL
Boneless, skinless chicken breast halves, chopped	4	4
All-purpose flour	6 tbsp.	100 mL
Salt	1 tsp.	5 mL
Pepper	¼ tsp.	1 mL
Milk	1½ cups	375 mL
Sherry (or alcohol-free sherry)	¼ cup	60 mL

Put first 5 ingredients into 3½ quart (3.5 L) slow cooker. Stir.

Scatter chicken over top.

Combine flour, salt and pepper in saucepan. Stir. Whisk in milk gradually until no lumps remain. Heat and stir until boiling and thickened. Mixture will be quite thick.

Stir in sherry. Pour over chicken. Cover. Cook on Low for 6 to 8 hours or on High for 3 to 4 hours. Stir. If chicken pieces have stuck together, break apart before serving. Makes 6 cups (1.5 L).

1 cup (250 mL): 171 Calories; 2 g Total Fat; 544 mg Sodium; 22 g Protein; 14 g Carbohydrate

SNAPPY CHICKEN

A bit sweet, a bit sour. Cranberries add a great flavor. Makes a dark sauce.

Sliced onion	1 cup	250 mL
Skinless chicken thighs	12	12
Whole cranberry sauce	1 cup	250 mL
Beef bouillon powder	1 tbsp.	15 mL
Cider vinegar	1 tsp.	5 mL
Prepared mustard	1 tsp.	5 mL
Salt	1½ tsp.	7 mL

(continued on next page)

Place onion in 5 quart (5 L) slow cooker. Arrange chicken thighs over onion.

Combine cranberry sauce, bouillon powder, vinegar, mustard and salt in bowl. Mix well. Spoon over chicken being sure to get some on every piece. Cover. Cook on Low for 6 to 8 hours or on High for 3 to 4 hours. Serves 4 to 6.

1 serving: 376 Calories; 8.6 g Total Fat; 1682 mg Sodium; 42 g Protein; 32 g Carbohydrate

ROAST CHICKEN

Final product is a tender, succulent chicken.

FRESH BREAD STUFFING

Hard margarine (butter browns too fast)	2 tbsp.	30 mL
Chopped onion	1 cup	250 mL
Diced celery	½ cup	125 mL
Salt	1 tsp.	5 mL
Pepper	¼ tsp.	1 mL
Parsley flakes	1 tsp.	5 mL
Poultry seasoning	¼-½ tsp.	1-2 mL
Bread slices, cubed (about 4 cups,1 L)	5	5

CHICKEN

Roasting chicken	3½ lbs.	1.6 kg
Liquid gravy browner	2 tsp.	10 mL

Gravy, page 48

Fresh Bread Stuffing: Melt margarine in frying pan. Add onion and celery. Sauté until soft. Remove from heat.

Mix in salt, pepper, parsley and poultry seasoning. Add bread cubes. Toss well. Wrap in foil, leaving an opening at top.

Chicken: Brush chicken with gravy browner. Place in 5 quart (5 L) slow cooker. Place foil pouch over chicken legs. Cover slow cooker. Cook on Low for 8 to 9 hours or on High for 4 to 4½ hours.

Make gravy with remaining juice from chicken. Stir stuffing before serving. Serves 6.

1 serving: 541 Calories; 35.4 g Total Fat; 1036 mg Sodium; 36 g Protein; 18 g Carbohydrate

Pictured on page 89.

CHICKEN STEW

Have this whole delicious meal ready and waiting. Juice may be left as is or it can be thickened.

Medium potatoes, cut bite size	4	4
Medium carrots, cut bite size	4	4
Chopped onion	1¼ cups	300 mL
Boneless, skinless chicken thighs (or drumsticks), cut bite size	1¼ lbs.	560 g
Hot water	2 cups	500 mL
Chicken bouillon powder	1 tbsp.	15 mL
Salt	1 tsp.	5 mL
Pepper	¼ tsp.	1 mL
Ground thyme	¼ tsp.	1 mL
Liquid gravy browner	½ tsp.	2 mL

Layer potato, carrot and onion in 5 quart (5 L) slow cooker. Lay chicken thighs on top.

Stir next 6 ingredients together in bowl. Pour over chicken. Cover. Cook on Low for 9 to 10 hours or on High for 4½ to 5 hours. Serves 6.

1 serving: 213 Calories; 4.2 g Total Fat; 896 mg Sodium; 21 g Protein; 23 g Carbohydrate; good source of Dietary Fiber

CHICKEN IN SAUCE

Makes lots of sauce. A green salad is the only thing needed to complete this meal.

Peeled baby carrots	30	30
Medium potatoes, cut up	4	4
Canned whole mushrooms, drained	10 oz.	284 mL
Chopped or sliced onion	½ cup	125 mL
Boneless, skinless chicken breast halves	6	6
Condensed cream of mushroom soup	10 oz.	284 mL
Chicken (or beef) bouillon powder	1 tsp.	5 mL
White (or alcohol-free) wine	¼ cup	60 mL
Envelope dry onion soup mix	1 × 1½ oz.	1 × 42 g
Salt (optional)	¼ tsp.	1 mL
Pepper	⅛ tsp.	0.5 mL

(continued on next page)

Arrange vegetables in layers in 5 quart (5 L) slow cooker. Lay chicken pieces over top.

Stir remaining 6 ingredients together well in bowl. Mix well. Spoon over chicken. Cover. Cook on Low for 10 to 12 hours or on High for 5 to 6 hours. Serves 6.

1 serving: 465 Calories; 9.1 g Total Fat; 2021 mg Sodium; 48 g Protein; 45 g Carbohydrate; good source of Dietary Fiber

CHICKEN DIVAN

Broccoli adds color and the sauce is "icing on the cake."

Broccoli florets	**3 cups**	**750 mL**
Skinless chicken breast halves	**4**	**4**
SAUCE		
All-purpose flour	**¼ cup**	**60 mL**
Chicken bouillon powder	**1 tbsp.**	**15 mL**
Salt	**½ tsp.**	**2 mL**
Pepper	**¼ tsp.**	**1 mL**
Milk	**2 cups**	**500 mL**
Grated Parmesan cheese	**¼ cup**	**60 mL**

Place broccoli in 5 quart (5 L) slow cooker. Lay chicken over top.

Sauce: Stir together flour, bouillon powder, salt and pepper in saucepan. Gradually whisk in milk until no lumps remain. Heat and stir until boiling and thickened. Remove from heat.

Stir in cheese. Pour over chicken. Cover. Cook on Low for 6 to 8 hours or on High for 3 to 4 hours. Serves 4.

1 serving: 271 Calories; 5.5 g Total Fat; 1111 mg Sodium; 38 g Protein; 17 g Carbohydrate

Paré Pointer

Old actors never die—they just lose their parts.

SESAME CHICKEN

Toasted sesame seeds darken even more and add a great flavor to chicken.

Skinless chicken thighs	3 lbs.	1.4 kg
Soy sauce	½ cup	125 mL
Sherry	2 tbsp.	30 mL
Brown sugar, packed	⅓ cup	75 mL
Garlic powder	¼ tsp.	1 mL
Ground ginger	¼ tsp.	1 mL
Ketchup	2 tbsp.	30 mL
Toasted sesame seeds	2 tbsp.	30 mL

Place chicken thighs in 3½ quart (3.5 L) slow cooker.

Combine remaining 7 ingredients in bowl. Mix well. Pour over chicken, being sure to get some sauce on every piece. Cover. Cook on Low for 6 to 8 hours or on High for 3 to 4 hours. Serves 4 to 6.

¼ recipe: 376 Calories; 10.1 g Total Fat; 2458 mg Sodium; 43 g Protein; 26 g Carbohydrate

COQ AU VIN

Wine flavor is evident in kohk-oh-VAHN. Served in fine restaurants.

Pearl onions, peeled (see Note)	24-36	24-36
Chicken parts, skin removed	3 lbs.	1.4 kg
Bacon slices, cooked crisp and crumbled	6	6
Small fresh mushrooms	2 cups	500 mL
Thinly sliced celery	½ cup	125 mL
Beef bouillon powder	2 tsp.	10 mL
Warm water	1½ cups	375 mL
Salt	½ tsp.	2 mL
Pepper	¼ tsp.	1 mL
Garlic powder	¼ tsp.	1 mL
Parsley flakes	1 tsp.	5 mL
Ground thyme	¼ tsp.	1 mL
Bay leaf	1	1
Red (or alcohol-free) wine	2 cups	500 mL
Gravy, page 48		

(continued on next page)

Place onion in 5 quart (5 L) slow cooker. Arrange chicken pieces, bacon, mushrooms and celery in order given over top.

Stir bouillon powder and warm water together in small bowl. Add salt, pepper, garlic powder, parsley flakes, thyme and bay leaf. Stir. Pour over chicken.

Add wine. Cover. Cook on Low for 8 to 10 hours or on High for 4 to 5 hours. Discard bay leaf.

Make gravy with remaining liquid. Serves 6.

Note: Allow 6 onions per person. To peel pearl onions easily, blanch in boiling water for about 2 minutes. Rinse in cold water and simply peel away skin.

1 serving: 266 Calories; 6.7 g Total Fat; 852 mg Sodium; 28 g Protein; 9 g Carbohydrate

SWEET AND SOUR CHICKEN

This has lots of sauce to go over rice or noodles.

Ketchup	2 tbsp.	30 mL
Water	1 cup	250 mL
White vinegar	½ cup	125 mL
Soy sauce	1 tbsp.	15 mL
Brown sugar, packed	1 cup	250 mL
Boneless, skinless chicken breasts (or thighs), cut bite size	1½ lbs.	680 g
Cornstarch	2 tbsp.	30 mL
Water	2 tbsp.	30 mL

Combine first 5 ingredients in 3½ quart (3.5 L) slow cooker. Stir.

Add chicken. Stir. Cover. Cook on Low for 6 to 8 hours or on High for 3 to 4 hours.

Combine cornstarch and second amount of water in small bowl. Stir into slow cooker. Cook on High, stirring often, for 15 to 20 minutes until thickened. For faster cooking, pour into saucepan. Heat on stove, stirring often, until thickened. Serves 6.

1 serving: 290 Calories; 1.4 g Total Fat; 328 mg Sodium; 27 g Protein; 43 g Carbohydrate

GINGER CHICKEN

Good ginger flavor with a wee bit of a bite. Add more cayenne pepper if desired.

Chicken parts, skin removed	3 lbs.	1.4 kg
Canned diced tomatoes	19 oz.	540 mL
Grated gingerroot	1 tbsp.	15 mL
Minute tapioca	2 tbsp.	30 mL
Garlic powder	1 tsp.	5 mL
Parsley flakes	1 tsp.	5 mL
Brown sugar, packed	1 tbsp.	15 mL
Cayenne pepper	1/4 tsp.	1 mL
Salt	1/2 tsp.	2 mL

Gravy, page 48

Arrange chicken in 3½ quart (3.5 L) slow cooker.

Combine remaining 8 ingredients in bowl. Stir well. Pour over chicken. Cover. Cook on Low for 7 to 8 hours or on High for 3½ to 4 hours.

Spoon off any fat. Make gravy with remaining juice. Serves 4 to 6.

¼ recipe: 276 Calories; 5.4 g Total Fat; 1030 mg Sodium; 38 g Protein; 18 g Carbohydrate

CHICKEN TETRAZZINI

A complete meal.

Chopped onion	1 cup	250 mL
Sliced fresh mushrooms	3 cups	750 mL
Chopped, boneless, skinless chicken (white or dark meat)	3 cups	750 mL
All-purpose flour	3 tbsp.	50 mL
Salt	1 tsp.	5 mL
Pepper	1/4 tsp.	1 mL
Chicken bouillon powder	1 tbsp.	15 mL
Water	1½ cups	375 mL
Skim evaporated milk	1 cup	250 mL
Sherry (or alcohol-free sherry)	3 tbsp.	50 mL
Spaghetti noodles, broken into short pieces	8 oz.	250 g
Grated Parmesan cheese, sprinkle		

(continued on next page)

Combine first 7 ingredients in 5 quart (5 L) slow cooker. Stir well to coat chicken with flour.

Pour water, evaporated milk and sherry into bowl. Stir. Pour over top. Cover. Cook on Low for 6 to 8 hours or on High for 3 to 4 hours.

Add noodles. Stir well to avoid sticking together. Push under liquid. Sprinkle with cheese. Cook on High for 15 to 20 minutes until tender. Makes 7 cups (1.75 L).

1 cup (250 mL): 296 Calories; 3.4 g Total Fat; 780 mg Sodium; 26 g Protein; 38 g Carbohydrate

CHICKEN & RICE

Canned chicken makes this an easy dish to prepare.

Chopped onion	1 cup	250 mL
Chopped fresh mushrooms	1 cup	250 mL
Medium green pepper, chopped	1	1
Uncooked converted rice	$3/4$ cup	175 mL
Canned flakes of chicken, with juice, broken up (or 2 cups, 500 mL, chopped cooked chicken)	2 × 6.5 oz.	2 × 184 g
Chicken bouillon powder	2 tsp.	10 mL
Warm water	1 cup	250 mL
Canned tomatoes, with juice, broken up	14 oz.	398 mL

Layer onion, mushrooms, green pepper, rice and chicken in 3½ quart (3.5 L) slow cooker.

Stir bouillon powder and warm water together in bowl. Add tomato. Stir. Pour over chicken. Cover. Cook on Low for 6 to 7 hours or on High for 3 to 3½ hours. Stir before serving. Makes 7 cups (1.75 L).

1 cup (250 mL): 185 Calories; 4.7 g Total Fat; 546 mg Sodium; 14 g Protein; 21 g Carbohydrate

Paré Pointer

One thing he can do better than anyone else is read his own handwriting.

CHICKEN CACCIATORE

Reddish in color. Excellent choice. Tomato adds its own flavor.

Chopped onion	1½ cups	375 mL
Chicken parts, skin removed	3 lbs.	1.4 kg
Canned tomatoes, with juice	14 oz.	398 mL
Tomato paste	5½ oz.	156 mL
Canned mushroom pieces, drained	10 oz.	284 mL
Bay leaf	1	1
Salt	1 tsp.	5 mL
Pepper	¼ tsp.	1 mL
Garlic powder	¼ tsp.	1 mL
Dried whole oregano	1 tsp.	5 mL
Dried sweet basil	½ tsp.	2 mL
White (or alcohol-free) wine	¼ cup	60 mL
Liquid gravy browner	½ tsp.	2 mL
Granulated sugar	1 tsp.	5 mL

Place onion and chicken in 3½ quart (3.5 L) slow cooker.

Combine next 12 ingredients in bowl. Stir. Pour over chicken. Cover. Cook on Low for 6 to 8 hours or on High for 3 to 4 hours. Discard bay leaf. Serves 4.

1 serving: 306 Calories; 5.7 g Total Fat; 1178 mg Sodium; 40 g Protein; 22 g Carbohydrate; excellent source of Dietary Fiber

Pictured on front cover.

QUICK FIX CHICKEN

A touch of sweetness with some onion flavor. Deep color with a nice glaze.

French dressing	½ cup	125 mL
Apricot jam	½ cup	125 mL
Envelope dry onion soup mix	1 × 1½ oz.	1 × 42 g
Chicken parts, skin removed	3 lbs.	1.4 kg

Mix first 3 ingredients in bowl.

Brush each piece of chicken with sauce. Arrange chicken in 3½ quart (3.5 L) slow cooker. Cover chicken with any remaining sauce. Cover. Cook on Low for 6 to 8 hours or on High 3 to 4 hours. Serves 6.

1 serving: 318 Calories; 12.4 g Total Fat; 1071 mg Sodium; 25 g Protein; 26 g Carbohydrate

"FRIED" CHICKEN

It looks and tastes like fried chicken.

All-purpose flour	$^1/_3$ cup	75 mL
Salt	1 tsp.	5 mL
Pepper	$^1/_4$ tsp.	1 mL
Paprika	1 tsp.	5 mL
Garlic powder (optional)	$^1/_4$ tsp.	1 mL
Chicken parts, skin removed	3 lbs.	1.4 kg

Gravy, page 48

Stir first 5 ingredients together in bowl. Pour into plastic or paper bag.

Shake 2 or 3 pieces of chicken at a time in bag to coat. Repeat for all pieces of chicken. Arrange on broiler tray. Broil on top rack in oven to brown quickly, not to cook. Transfer to $3^1/_2$ quart (3.5 L) slow cooker. Cover. Cook on Low for 8 to 10 hours or on High for 4 to 5 hours.

Make gravy with remaining juice. Serves 6.

1 serving: 171 Calories; 3.4 g Total Fat; 763 mg Sodium; 25 g Protein; 8 g Carbohydrate

LEMONADE CHICKEN

A sweet citrus flavor. Lots of liquid to make gravy with.

Frozen concentrated lemonade, thawed	$^1/_2$ × $12^1/_2$ oz.	$^1/_2$ × 355 mL
Brown sugar, packed	3 tbsp.	50 mL
Ketchup	3 tbsp.	50 mL
White vinegar	1 tbsp.	15 mL
Liquid gravy browner	1 tsp.	5 mL
Boneless, skinless chicken breast halves	6	6

Gravy, page 48

Stir first 5 ingredients in bowl.

Arrange chicken pieces in bottom of $3^1/_2$ quart (3.5 L) slow cooker, overlapping if necessary. Pour lemonade mixture over all. Cover. Cook on Low for 8 to 10 hours or on High for 4 to 5 hours.

Make gravy with remaining liquid. Serves 6.

1 serving: 244 Calories; 1.7 g Total Fat; 433 mg Sodium; 28 g Protein; 29 g Carbohydrate

Pictured on page 107.

CORNISH GAME HENS

Certainly a no-fuss way to cook these. Prepare commercial stuffing separately to serve along side.

SESAME COATING

Ketchup	1 tbsp.	15 mL
White vinegar	1½ tsp.	7 mL
Soy sauce	1½ tsp.	7 mL
Brown sugar, packed	1 tbsp.	15 mL
Ground ginger	⅛ tsp.	0.5 mL
Toasted sesame seeds	1 tbsp.	15 mL
Cornish hens (about 1¾ lbs., 790 g, each), see Note	2	2

Gravy, page 48

Sesame Coating: Stir first 6 ingredients together in small bowl.

Spread coating over each Cornish hen. Place side by side in 3½ quart (3.5 L) or 5 quart (5 L) slow cooker. Cover. Cook on Low for 7 to 8 hours or on High for 3½ to 4 hours.

Make gravy with remaining juice from Cornish hens. Serves 4.

1 serving: 664 Calories; 46.4 g Total Fat; 718 mg Sodium; 50 g Protein; 9 g Carbohydrate

Note: Double Sesame Coating to cook 4 Cornish hens. Place each Cornish hen in 5 quart (5 L) slow cooker, neck end touching bottom. To cook in 3½ quart (3.5 L) slow cooker, pile 2 Cornish hens on top of first 2. Bottom hens will cook faster so, if possible, reverse positions at half-time.

1. Beef In Wine, page 40
2. Stuffed Baked Potatoes, page 109
3. Chick Pea Stew, page 21
4. Chocolate Fondue, page 145
5. French Onion Soup, page 133
6. Apple Punch, page 51

Props Courtesy Of: Creations By Design; Sears Canada Inc; Stokes; The Bay

CHICKEN MARENGO

Spaghetti sauce mix gives a flavor boost.

Canned sliced mushrooms, drained	10 oz.	284 mL
Sliced onion	1 cup	250 mL
Chicken parts, skin removed	3 lbs.	1.4 kg
Canned tomatoes, with juice, broken up	14 oz.	398 mL
Envelope spaghetti sauce mix	1 x 1½ oz.	1 x 43 g

Arrange mushrooms and onion in 5 quart (5 L) slow cooker. Lay chicken pieces over top.

Stir tomato and spaghetti sauce mix together in bowl. Pour over top of chicken. Cover. Cook on Low for 8 to 10 hours or on High for 4 to 5 hours. Serves 6.

1 serving: 179 Calories; 3.6 g Total Fat; 907 mg Sodium; 26 g Protein; 10 g Carbohydrate

DRUMSTICK BAKE

Browned drumsticks with nice gravy to spoon over mashed potato.

Chicken drumsticks, skin removed	12	12
Condensed cream of chicken soup	10 oz.	284 mL
Onion flakes	2 tbsp.	30 mL
Liquid gravy browner	½ tsp.	2 mL

Arrange drumsticks in 3½ quart (3.5 L) slow cooker.

Combine soup, onion flakes and gravy browner in bowl. Stir well. Spoon over chicken. Cover. Cook on Low for 6 to 7 hours or on High for 3 to 3½ hours. Serves 4 to 6.

¼ recipe: 303 Calories; 10.8 g Total Fat; 778 mg Sodium; 41 g Protein; 9 g Carbohydrate

Paré Pointer

Old bacteriologists never die—they go out to Pasteur.

CHICKEN CURRY

A pleasant curry flavor. You can adjust the amount of curry to make it milder or hotter. Lots of broth.

Chopped onion	1 cup	250 mL
Medium tomatoes, diced	2	2
Medium green pepper, chopped	1	1
Hot water	4 cups	1 L
Curry powder	3 tbsp.	50 mL
Chicken bouillon powder	4 tsp.	20 mL
Ketchup	1 tbsp.	15 mL
Salt	1 tsp.	5 mL
Boneless, skinless chicken breast halves (or thighs)	1½ lbs.	680 g

Put onion into 5 quart (5 L) slow cooker. Scatter tomato and green pepper over onion.

Stir next 5 ingredients together in bowl. Pour over vegetables.

Arrange chicken pieces over top. Cover. Cook on Low for 8 to 10 hours or on High for 4 to 5 hours. Transfer chicken to platter. Remove vegetables with slotted spoon and place beside chicken. Pour broth into gravy boat to serve over rice, noodles or mashed potatoes. Serves 6.

1 serving: 167 Calories; 2.4 g Total Fat; 1000 mg Sodium; 28 g Protein; 8 g Carbohydrate

CRANBERRY SAUCE

Gorgeous colored whole cranberry sauce. Needs no attention.

Granulated sugar	2 cups	500 mL
Boiling water	1 cup	250 mL
Fresh (or frozen) cranberries	4 cups	1 L

Stir sugar and boiling water together in 3½ quart (3.5 L) slow cooker.

Add cranberries. Cover. Cook on High for about 1½ hours until most of the berries have popped. Cool. Makes 3½ cups (875 mL).

2 tbsp. (30 mL): 62 Calories; trace Total Fat; trace Sodium; trace Protein; 16 g Carbohydrate

Pictured on page 89.

Golden chicken in golden sauce. Great with rice.

Large egg, fork-beaten	1	1
Salt	½ tsp.	2 mL
Pepper	¼ tsp.	1 mL
Fine dry bread crumbs	½ cup	125 mL
Chicken bouillon powder	2 tsp.	10 mL
Ground chicken	1½ lbs.	680 g
Canned pineapple tidbits, with juice	14 oz.	398 mL
White vinegar	⅓ cup	75 mL
Ketchup	2 tsp.	10 mL
Soy sauce	2 tsp.	10 mL
Chicken bouillon powder	1 tsp.	5 mL
Brown sugar, packed	⅓ cup	75 mL
Medium green pepper, diced into ¾ inch (2 cm) pieces	1	1
Chopped green onion	⅓ cup	75 mL
Water	⅔ cup	150 mL
Cornstarch	3 tbsp.	50 mL

Place first 5 ingredients in bowl. Stir well.

Add ground chicken. Mix. Shape into 1½ inch (3.8 cm) balls. Arrange on broiler tray. Broil, turning once, until browned. This will take about 4 to 5 minutes per side. Place meatballs in 3½ quart (3.5 L) slow cooker.

Combine next 8 ingredients in saucepan.

Mix water and cornstarch in small cup. Add to saucepan. Heat and stir until boiling and thickened. Pour over meatballs. (If preparing the evening before, cool sauce thoroughly before pouring over chicken and placing in the refrigerator.) Cover. Cook on Low for 4 to 5 hours or on High for 2 to 2½ hours. Makes 30 meatballs.

3 meatballs (with sauce and veggies): 178 Calories; 2.8 g Total Fat; 518 mg Sodium; 16 g protein; 22 g Carbohydrate

Paré Pointer

One food strikes terror in Dracula's heart. Stake!

TURKEY DRUMS

Economical, moist and tasty.

Turkey drumsticks (about ³/₄ lbs., 340 g, each)	**2**	**2**
Beef bouillon powder	2 tsp.	10 mL
Onion powder	¼ tsp.	1 mL
Seasoning salt	½ tsp.	2 mL
Brown sugar, packed	¼ cup	60 mL
Ketchup	1 tbsp.	15 mL
Gravy, page 48		

Place drumsticks, meaty side down, in 3¹/₂ quart (3.5 L) slow cooker.

Combine next 5 ingredients in bowl. Mix well. Spread over top. Cover. Cook on Low for 7 to 9 hours or on High for 3¹/₂ to 4¹/₂ hours. Remove skin before serving if desired.

Make gravy with remaining juice from turkey. Serves 2.

1 serving: 438 Calories; 9.9 g Total Fat; 1889 mg Sodium; 47 g Protein; 38 g Carbohydrate

TURKEY ROLL

Makes any meal seem quite festive.

Boneless turkey roll	**2¹/₂ lbs.**	**1.1 kg**
Stuffing, page 131		
Gravy, page 48		

Place turkey roll in 3¹/₂ quart (3.5 L) slow cooker.

Prepare stuffing. Wrap in foil, leaving an opening at top. Place over turkey. Cover slow cooker. Cook on Low for 8 to 10 hours or on High for 4 to 5 hours.

Make gravy with remaining juice from turkey. Serves 6.

1 serving: 579 Calories; 14.8 g Total Fat; 1730 mg Sodium; 52 g Protein; 56 g Carbohydrate

The perfect solution when oven space is scarce.

Chopped celery	**1 cup**	**250 mL**
Chopped onion	**1 cup**	**250 mL**
Parsley flakes	**1 tbsp.**	**15 mL**
Poultry seasoning	**2 tsp.**	**10 mL**
Salt	**1 tsp.**	**5 mL**
Pepper	**¼ tsp.**	**1 mL**
Dry bread cubes	**10 cups**	**2.5 L**
Hard margarine (or butter)	**¼ cup**	**60 mL**
Chicken bouillon powder	**1 tbsp.**	**15 mL**
Hot water	**1½ cups**	**375 mL**

Put first 6 ingredients into large bowl. Stir well.

Add bread cubes. Stir.

Combine margarine, bouillon powder and hot water in separate bowl. Stir to melt margarine and dissolve bouillon powder. Pour over bread cube mixture. Turn into 5 quart (5 L) slow cooker. Cover. Cook on Low for 5 to 6 hours. If you prefer a more moist stuffing, add a bit more hot water and stir. Makes 8 cups (2 L).

½ cup (125 mL): 135 Calories; 4.4 g Total Fat; 522 mg Sodium; 4 g Protein; 20 g Carbohydrate

Paré Pointer

Old taxis usually end up in the old cabb-age home.

TURKEY LOAF

Serve for supper and use leftovers for sandwiches. This loaf cuts so well for sandwiches.

Large egg, fork-beaten	1	1
Finely chopped onion	½ cup	125 mL
Salt	½ tsp.	2 mL
Pepper	¼ tsp.	1 mL
Ground thyme	¼ tsp.	1 mL
Prepared horseradish	1 tsp.	5 mL
Quick-cooking rolled oats (not instant)	½ cup	125 mL
Ground turkey	1½ lbs.	680 g
Ketchup	2 tbsp.	30 mL
Prepared mustard	1 tsp.	5 mL

Combine first 7 ingredients in bowl. Mix well.

Add ground turkey. Mix. Turn into greased 3½ quart (3.5 L) slow cooker.

Mix ketchup and mustard in small cup. Spread over top. Cover. Cook on Low for 5 to 6 hours or on High for 2½ to 3 hours. Serves 6.

1 serving: 177 Calories; 3.2 g Total Fat; 388 mg Sodium; 28 g Protein; 8 g Carbohydrate

TURKEY ROAST

Sliced white meat with an apple-flavored fruity sauce.

Medium cooking apples, peeled and sliced (such as McIntosh)	2	2
Whole cranberry sauce	½ cup	125 mL
Boneless, skinless turkey breast roast	2⅛ lbs.	1 kg
Liquid gravy browner	1 tsp.	5 mL

Arrange apple slices in 5 quart (5 L) slow cooker. Dot cranberry sauce here and there over apple.

Brush roast with gravy browner. Place on top of apple mixture. Cover. Cook on Low for 8 to 9 hours or on High for 4 to 4½ hours. Serve with remaining juice mixture. Serves 6.

1 serving: 242 Calories; 1.3 g Total Fat; 114 mg Sodium; 40 g Protein; 16 g Carbohydrate

MEATLESS SOUPS

It's easy to turn a meat soup recipe into a meatless soup recipe. Simply omit the meat and taste for seasoning. Chicken, beef or vegetable bouillon powder will add strength to the flavor. Taste for salt and pepper. Other popular spices are oregano, basil, garlic powder, onion powder and thyme. A touch of gravy browner or ketchup will add color.

FRENCH ONION SOUP

Simple and just like you would have when dining out.

Quartered and thinly sliced white onion (about 1½ lbs., 680 g)	4¼ cups	1 L
Water	4 cups	1 L
Beef bouillon powder	4 tsp.	20 mL
French bread slices, cut to fit	4	4
Grated mozzarella cheese	1 cup	250 mL
Grated Parmesan cheese, sprinkle		

Combine first 3 ingredients in 3½ quart (3.5 L) slow cooker. Cover. Cook on Low for 8 to 10 hours or on High for 4 to 5 hours.

Ladle soup into bowls. Place 1 slice of bread in each bowl. Divide mozzarella cheese and sprinkle over each slice. Sprinkle with Parmesan cheese. Broil until cheese is bubbly and golden brown. If preferred, bread with cheese may be broiled separately, then added to each bowl. Serves 4.

1 cup (250 mL): 211 Calories; 8.3 g Total Fat; 809 mg Sodium; 10 g Protein; 25 g Carbohydrate

Pictured on page 125.

Paré Pointer

Old lawyers never die—they just lose their appeal.

CHICKEN VEGETABLE SOUP

A colorful soup in a clear broth. Lots of chicken.

Boneless, skinless chicken breast halves, diced	3	3
Chopped onion	1 cup	250 mL
Thinly sliced carrot	1⅓ cups	325 mL
Diced celery	½ cup	125 mL
Diced turnip	½ cup	125 mL
Diced potato	2 cups	500 mL
Chicken bouillon powder	1 tbsp.	15 mL
Salt	1 tsp.	5 mL
Pepper	¼ tsp.	1 mL
Ground thyme	¼ tsp.	1 mL
Water	4 cups	1 L
Liquid gravy browner, to color slightly (optional)		

Place first 11 ingredients in 5 quart (5 L) slow cooker. Stir. Cover. Cook on Low for 8 to 10 hours or on High for 4 to 5 hours. If vegetables are large and not quite tender, turn heat to High for a few minutes.

Add gravy browner just before serving. Taste for salt and pepper, adding more if needed. Makes 8 cups (2 L).

1 cup (250 mL): 105 Calories; 0.9 g Total Fat; 635 mg Sodium; 12 g Protein; 12 g Carbohydrate

SPLIT PEA SOUP

Very attractive. Carrot adds color. A dandy green pea soup.

Dried split green peas	2 cups	500 mL
Canned flakes of ham, with liquid, broken up (or 1 cup, 250 mL, diced ham)	6.5 oz.	184 g
Medium carrot, thinly sliced or diced	1	1
Diced celery	½ cup	125 mL
Finely chopped onion	1 cup	250 mL
Salt	½ tsp.	2 mL
Pepper	¼ tsp.	1 mL
Parsley flakes	1 tsp.	5 mL
Chicken bouillon powder	1 tbsp.	15 mL
Ground thyme	¼ tsp.	1 mL
Water	5 cups	1.25 L

(continued on next page)

Combine all 11 ingredients in 3½ quart (3.5 L) slow cooker. Stir. Cover. Cook on Low for 8 to 10 hours or on High for 4 to 5 hours. Makes 7¾ cups (1.9 L).

1 cup (250 mL): 265 Calories; 5.4 g Total Fat; 771 mg Sodium; 18 g Protein; 37 g Carbohydrate; excellent source of Dietary Fiber

Pictured on page 143.

BEEF MINESTRONE

When your day away from home is long, this will be ready and waiting for your return.

Beef stew meat, diced small	½ lb.	225 g
Canned tomatoes, with juice, broken up	14 oz.	398 mL
Chopped onion	1 cup	250 mL
Grated cabbage	1 cup	250 mL
Medium carrot, diced or thinly sliced	1	1
Small zucchini with peel (about 7 inches, 18 cm), cubed	1	1
Medium potato, diced	1	1
Parsley flakes	1 tsp.	5 mL
Garlic powder	¼ tsp.	1 mL
Dried sweet basil	¼ tsp.	1 mL
Dried whole oregano	¼ tsp.	1 mL
Salt	1½ tsp.	7 mL
Pepper	¼ tsp.	1 mL
Water	4 cups	1 L
Canned kidney beans, drained	14 oz.	398 mL
Uncooked elbow macaroni	½ cup	125 mL
Grated Parmesan cheese, sprinkle		

Combine first 14 ingredients in 3½ quart (3.5 L) or 5 quart (5 L) slow cooker. Stir well. Cover. Cook on Low for 10 to 12 hours or on High for 5 to 6 hours.

Turn heat to High. Add kidney beans and macaroni. Cook for 15 to 20 minutes until macaroni is tender.

Sprinkle with cheese to serve. Makes 10½ cups (2.6 L).

1 cup (250 mL): 97 Calories; 1 g Total Fat; 514 mg Sodium; 7 g Protein; 15 g Carbohydrate; good source of Dietary Fiber

Pictured on front cover.

BEAN SOUP

Brownish color with tomato adding a bit of color. Thick soup with a good flavor. Contains canned ham. Simple to make.

Dried navy beans (1 lb., 454 g)	2¹/₃ cups	575 mL
Chopped onion	1¹/₄ cups	300 mL
Garlic clove, minced (or ¹/₄ tsp.,1 mL, powder)	1	1
Canned flakes of ham, with liquid, broken up (or 1 cup, 250 mL, diced ham)	6.5 oz.	184 g
Canned tomatoes, with juice, broken up	14 oz.	398 mL
Water	6 cups	1.5 L
Salt	1 tsp.	5 mL
Pepper	¹/₄ tsp.	1 mL

Measure all 8 ingredients into 5 quart (5 L) slow cooker. Stir well. Cover. Cook on Low for 8 to 10 hours or on High for 4 to 5 hours. Taste for salt and pepper, adding more if needed. Makes 9²/₃ cups (2.4 L).

1 cup (250 mL): 232 Calories; 4.4 g Total Fat; 616 mg Sodium; 15 g Protein; 35 g Carbohydrate; good source of Dietary Fiber

BEEF BARLEY SOUP

A hearty soup.

Beef stew meat, diced small	1 lb.	454 g
Sliced or chopped carrot	1¹/₄ cups	300 mL
Chopped onion	1¹/₄ cups	300 mL
Chopped celery	³/₄ cup	175 mL
Water	5 cups	1.25 L
Parsley flakes	1 tsp.	5 mL
Pepper	¹/₄ tsp.	1 mL
Granulated sugar	1 tsp.	5 mL
Beef bouillon powder	2 tbsp.	30 mL
Pearl barley	¹/₂ cup	125 mL
Tomato sauce	2 × 7.5 oz.	2 × 213 mL

Place all 11 ingredients in 5 quart (5 L) slow cooker. Stir. Cover. Cook on Low for 8 to 10 hours or on High for 4 to 5 hours. Makes 10¹/₄ cups (2.5 L).

1 cup (250 mL): 113 Calories; 1.8 g Total Fat; 637 mg Sodium; 9 g Protein; 16 g Carbohydrate; good source of Dietary Fiber

BEEF VEGETABLE SOUP

Rich color and a full-meal soup. Serve with garlic bread or crusty rolls.

Lean ground beef	1 lb.	454 g
Canned diced tomatoes	14 oz.	398 mL
Chopped onion	1 cup	250 mL
Frozen mixed vegetables	10 oz.	300 g
Thinly sliced or diced carrot	1 cup	250 mL
Diced potato	1½ cups	375 mL
Diced celery	½ cup	125 mL
Condensed tomato soup	10 oz.	284 mL
Water	3 cups	750 mL
Granulated sugar	1 tsp.	5 mL
Salt	½ tsp.	2 mL
Pepper	¼ tsp.	1 mL
Liquid gravy browner	1 tsp.	5 mL

Scramble-fry ground beef In non-stick frying pan until no longer pink. Drain well.

Combine ground beef and remaining 12 ingredients in 5 quart (5 L) slow cooker. Stir well. Cover. Cook on Low for 9 to 10 hours or on High for 4½ to 5 hours. Makes 10⅔ cups (2.68 L).

1 cup (250 mL): 141 Calories; 4.2 g Total Fat; 439 mg Sodium; 10 g Protein; 17 g Carbohydrate

SIMPLE BEAN SOUP

A good soup born of convenience food you can have ready in record time.

Canned navy beans	2 × 14 oz.	2 × 398 mL
Canned flakes of ham, with liquid, broken up (or 1 cup, 250 mL, diced ham)	6.5 oz.	184 g
Chopped onion	1½ cups	375 mL
Beef bouillon powder	1 tbsp.	15 mL
Warm water	2½ cups	625 mL
Ketchup	1 tbsp.	15 mL

Combine all 6 ingredients in 3½ quart (3.5 L) slow cooker. Stir. Cover. Cook on Low for 8 to 10 hours or on High for 4 to 5 hours. Makes 7 cups (1.75 L).

1 cup (250 mL): 225 Calories; 5.7 g Total Fat; 1208 mg Sodium; 14 g Protein; 30 g Carbohydrate; good source of Dietary Fiber

EASY BEAN SOUP

Excellent and easy-to-make soup. Vegetables add color.

Canned brown beans with molasses	2 x 14 oz.	2 x 398 mL
Canned flakes of ham, with liquid, broken up (or 1 cup, 250 mL, diced ham)	6.5 oz.	184 g
Chopped onion	¾ cup	175 mL
Chopped celery	½ cup	125 mL
Medium carrots, thinly sliced or diced	2	2
Medium tomatoes, diced	2	2
Garlic powder	¼ tsp.	1 mL
Chicken bouillon powder	2 tbsp.	30 mL
Water	4 cups	1 L
Dried sweet basil	¼ tsp.	1 mL
Granulated sugar	1 tsp.	5 mL

Combine all 11 ingredients in 3½ quart (3.5 L) slow cooker. Stir. Cover. Cook on Low for 8 to 10 hours or on High for 4 to 5 hours. Makes 9 cups (2.25 L).

1 cup (250 mL): 165 Calories; 4.8 g Total Fat; 1104 mg Sodium; 9 g Protein; 25 g Carbohydrate; excellent source of Dietary Fiber

Pictured on page 89.

CHICKEN STOCK

Easy to make soup from scratch, beginning with stock. No need to keep an eye on this.

Chicken drumsticks (or meaty backs and necks), see Note	1 lb.	454 g
Medium onion, chopped	1	1
Medium carrot, chopped	1	1
Chopped celery	1 cup	250 mL
Small bay leaf	1	1
Parsley flakes	1 tsp.	5 mL
Whole cloves	4	4
Salt	2 tsp.	10 mL
Pepper	½ tsp.	2 mL
Ground thyme	¼ tsp.	1 mL
Liquid gravy browner (optional)	½ tsp.	2 mL

Water, to cover

(continued on next page)

Place drumsticks in 3½ quart (3.5 L) slow cooker. Add next 10 ingredients.

Pour water over all. Cover. Cook on Low for 8 to 10 hours or on High for 4 to 5 hours. Skim if needed. Remove chicken and take off skin. Chop chicken and reserve for soup. Strain broth. Chill. Spoon off fat from top. Makes 4⅓ cups (1 L) stock.

1 cup (250 mL): 9 Calories; 0.2 g Total Fat; 1367 mg Sodium; trace Protein; 2 g Carbohydrate

Note: To strengthen flavor, chicken bouillon cubes or powder may be added. If using bones to make soup, browning bones before placing in slow cooker also adds to the flavor. You may choose to cook bones without the vegetables.

BEEF STOCK

The slow cooker is ideal for getting all the flavor from soup bones. Takes no minding.

Meaty beef soup bone, cut into pieces (see Note)	3 lbs.	1.4 kg
Medium carrots, chopped	2	2
Medium onion, chopped	1	1
Celery ribs, chopped	2	2
Parsley flakes (or ⅓ cup, 75 mL, fresh)	4 tsp.	20 mL
Whole peppercorns	6	6
Bay leaf	1	1
Salt	1 tsp.	5 mL
Ground thyme	⅛ tsp.	0.5 mL
Water, to cover (approximately)	7 cups	1.75 L

Roast bones in small uncovered roaster in 350°F (175°C) oven for about 1 hour until brown. Transfer to slow cooker.

Add remaining 9 ingredients. Stir. Cover. Cook on Low for 10 to 12 hours or on High for 5 to 6 hours. Remove bones. Cut off beef. Chop and reserve to use in soup. Discard bones. Strain stock into container. Chill. Spoon off fat from top. Discard vegetables. Use in any beef soup recipe. Makes 5¼ cups (1.3 L).

Note: For a more flavorful stock, have your butcher saw beef bone into pieces.

1 cup (250 mL): 7 Calories; trace Total Fat; 524 mg Sodium; trace Protein; 2 g Carbohydrate

BEEF AND SPLIT PEA SOUP

Makes a large batch. Make half the recipe for a small slow cooker. Chunky, colorful and thick. Freezes well.

Lean ground beef	1 lb.	454 g
Chopped onion	1 cup	250 mL
Yellow split peas	½ cup	125 mL
Pearl barley	½ cup	125 mL
Uncooked long grain converted rice	½ cup	125 mL
Parsley flakes	1 tsp.	5 mL
Liquid gravy browner	½ tsp.	2 mL
Canned tomatoes, with juice, broken up	2 × 14 oz.	2 × 398 mL
Condensed tomato soup	10 oz.	284 mL
Beef bouillon powder	1 tbsp.	15 mL
Salt	2 tsp.	10 mL
Pepper	½ tsp.	2 mL
Water	12 cups	3 L
Ground thyme	¼ tsp.	1 mL
Uncooked tiny shell pasta	2 cups	500 mL

Scramble-fry ground beef in non-stick frying pan until no longer pink. Drain well.

Combine next 13 ingredients in 5 quart (5 L) slow cooker. Add ground beef. Stir. Cover. Cook on Low for 9 to 11 hours or on High for 4½ to 5½ hours.

Add pasta. Stir. Cover. Cook on High for 15 to 20 minutes until pasta is tender. Makes 17⅓ cups (4.3 L).

1 cup (250 mL): 177 Calories; 3 g Total Fat; 631 mg Sodium; 10 g Protein; 28 g Carbohydrate

Paré Pointer

One worm to another: "I saw my first robin today—and just in time too!"

Meaty, colorful and a meal in itself. Sour cream makes it authentic.

Medium beets, peeled and cut into thin strips	2	2
Medium carrot, chopped	1	1
Medium onion, chopped	1	1
Coarsely shredded cabbage, packed	1 cup	250 mL
Medium potato, chopped	1	1
Chopped celery	½ cup	125 mL
Water, to cover (approximately), see Note	6 cups	1.5 L
Beef bouillon powder	2 tbsp.	30 mL
Boiling water	½ cup	125 mL
Lemon juice	2 tsp.	10 mL
Dill weed	½ tsp.	2 mL
Salt	2 tsp.	10 mL
Pepper	½ tsp.	2 mL
Lean ground beef	1 lb.	454 g
Frozen peas	1 cup	250 mL
Canned cut green beans, drained	14 oz.	398 mL
Light sour cream, dollop for each bowl (optional, but good)		

Place first 7 ingredients in 5 quart (5 L) slow cooker.

Stir bouillon powder into boiling water in bowl. Add lemon juice, dill weed, salt and pepper. Stir. Pour into slow cooker. Stir.

Scramble-fry ground beef in non-stick frying pan until no longer pink. Drain. Add to slow cooker.

Sprinkle peas and green beans over top. Cover. Cook on Low for 10 to 12 hours or on High for 5 to 6 hours.

Stir before serving. Add a dollop of sour cream to each bowl. Makes 13 cups (3.25 L).

Note: To shorten cooking time by at least 1 hour on Low, use boiling water.

1 cup (250 mL): 86 Calories; 3.2 g Total Fat; 763 mg Sodium; 8 g Protein; 7 g Carbohydrate

Pictured on page 71.

SIMMERING POTPOURRI

To add a subtle aroma in your home, start potpourri simmering one hour before your guests arrive and continue throughout the evening.

Dried lavender leaves	1 cup	250 mL
Dried rose petals	4 cups	1 L
Anise seed	1 tsp.	5 mL
Ground nutmeg	1 tbsp.	15 mL
Whole cloves	1 tbsp.	15 mL
Cinnamon stick (2 inches, 5 cm, in length), broken up and crushed in plastic bag	1	1
Crushed benzoin fixative	1 tbsp.	15 mL
Drops of jasmine oil	5	5
Drops of patchouli oil	5	5
Drops of rose geranium oil	5	5
Drops of rosemary oil	5	5

Mix all ingredients in a large bowl. Place in a large opaque container, or in a glass container in a dark cupboard. Let stand for 1 month to season before using. Makes about 5 cups (1.25 L). To use, fill slow cooker half full with water. Add 1 to 2 cups (250 to 500 mL) potpourri. Heat on Low with the lid off.

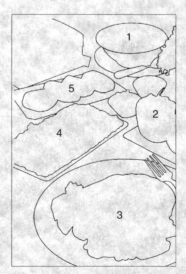

Props Courtesy Of: Scona Clayworks; Stokes; The Bay; Wicker World

CHOCOLATE FONDUE

The ultimate! Smooth and delicious. A favorite to be sure. Use fondue forks to spear and dip maraschino cherries, whole strawberries, banana chunks, large marshmallows, or cake cubes.

Semisweet chocolate chips	2½ cups	625 mL
Skim evaporated milk	½ cup	125 mL
Jar of marshmallow cream	7 oz.	200 g

Put first 3 ingredients into 3½ quart (3.5 L) slow cooker. Cover. Cook on Low for 1 hour until quite warm. Stir well at half-time. Makes a generous 2⅓ cups (575 mL).

2 tbsp. (30 mL) fondue: 156 Calories; 8.3 g Total Fat; 20 mg Sodium; 2 g Protein; 22 g Carbohydrate

Pictured on page 125.

CHOCOLATE SUNDAE: Spoon hot Chocolate Fondue sauce over scoops of vanilla, strawberry or chocolate ice cream. Also excellent used as a topping for Marbled Cheesecake, page 80.

CHEESE FONDUE

Take your slow cooker and a loaf of French bread on a trip to the mountains and enjoy this in your hotel room or cabin. Cook on Low to avoid cheese going stringy. At home, dip broccoli florets or cauliflower florets (cooked tender crisp), or warmed wiener chunks into sauce.

Condensed Cheddar cheese soup	10 oz.	284 mL
Grated Monterey Jack cheese	1 cup	250 mL
Grated Parmesan cheese	2 tbsp.	30 mL
Chopped chives	2 tbsp.	30 mL
Garlic powder	⅛ tsp.	0.5 mL
Cayenne pepper	⅛ tsp.	0.5 mL
White wine (or alcohol-free wine or milk)	¼ cup	60 mL

Place all ingredients in 3½ quart (3.5 L) slow cooker. Stir well. Cover. Cook on Low for 2 to 2½ hours until quite warm. Makes 1¾ cups (425 mL).

2 tbsp. (30 mL) fondue: 63 Calories; 4.4 g Total Fat; 215 mg Sodium; 3 g Protein; 2 g Carbohydrate

RATATOUILLE

This ra-tuh-TOO-ee is made up of six different vegetables.

Canned tomatoes, with juice, broken up (or 4 fresh medium tomatoes, diced)	19 oz.	540 mL
Small eggplant, with peel, cut into ½ inch (12 mm) cubes	1	1
Finely chopped onion	1 cup	250 mL
Chopped celery	1 cup	250 mL
Medium green or red pepper, chopped	1	1
Ketchup (or chili sauce)	¼ cup	60 mL
Granulated sugar	2 tsp.	10 mL
Sliced zucchini, with peel (¼ inch, 6 mm, thick)	3 cups	750 mL
Parsley flakes	1 tsp.	5 mL
Salt	½ tsp.	2 mL
Pepper	⅛ tsp.	0.5 mL
Garlic powder	¼ tsp.	1 mL
Dried whole oregano	½ tsp.	2 mL
Dried sweet basil	½ tsp.	2 mL

Measure all 14 ingredients into a 5 quart (5 L) slow cooker. Stir. Cover. Cook on Low for 8 to 9 hours or on High for 4 to 4½ hours. Makes 6½ cups (1.6 L).

1 cup (250 mL): 64 Calories; 0.5 g Total Fat; 500 mg Sodium; 2 g Protein; 15 g Carbohydrate

CREAMED CABBAGE

In a delicious cream sauce.

Medium cabbage, finely chopped	1	1
Finely chopped onion	½ cup	125 mL
Water	¼ cup	60 mL
All-purpose flour	3 tbsp.	50 mL
Chicken bouillon powder	½ tsp.	2 mL
Salt	½ tsp.	2 mL
Pepper	⅛ tsp.	0.5 mL
Milk	2 cups	500 mL
TOPPING		
Hard margarine (or butter)	1 tbsp.	15 mL
Fine dry bread crumbs	¼ cup	60 mL

(continued on next page)

Place cabbage, onion and water in 5 quart (5 L) slow cooker. Cover. Cook on Low for 4 to 6 hours or on High for 2 to 3 hours. Drain.

Stir next 4 ingredients in saucepan. Whisk in milk gradually until no lumps remain. Heat and stir until boiling and thickened. Pour over cabbage. Stir.

Topping: Melt margarine in saucepan. Stir in bread crumbs. Heat and stir until browned. Sprinkle over cabbage mixture before serving. Makes 4 cups (1 L).

½ cup (125 mL): 104 Calories; 2.8 g Total Fat; 317 mg Sodium; 5 g Protein; 17 g Carbohydrate; good source of Dietary Fiber

STUFFED PEPPERS

Green peppers with red soup topping. Filling is mild and very delicious.

Boiling water	¼ cup	60 mL
Instant white rice	¼ cup	60 mL
Finely chopped onion	¼ cup	60 mL
Grated carrot	¼ cup	60 mL
Kernel corn, frozen or canned	¼ cup	60 mL
Worcestershire sauce	½ tsp.	2 mL
Prepared horseradish	½ tsp.	2 mL
Salt	½ tsp.	2 mL
Pepper	⅛ tsp.	0.5 mL
Lean ground beef	½ lb.	225 g
Medium green peppers, tops cut off	4	4
Condensed tomato soup	10 oz.	284 mL

Pour boiling water over rice in bowl. Cover. Let stand for 5 minutes.

Add next 8 ingredients. Mix well.

Stuff peppers with rice mixture. Place in 5 quart (5 L) slow cooker.

Spoon soup over top and around peppers. Cover. Cook on Low for 7 to 9 hours or on High for 3½ to 4½ hours. Serves 4.

1 serving: 234 Calories; 9.9 g Total Fat; 915 mg Sodium; 14 g Protein; 24 g Carbohydrate

Pictured on page 143.

ASPARAGUS BAKE

Retains shape and color.

Fresh asparagus	1 lb.	454 g
All-purpose flour	1½ tbsp.	25 mL
Salt	¼ tsp.	1 mL
Pepper	1/16 tsp.	0.5 mL
Skim evaporated milk	¾ cup	175 mL
Grated sharp Cheddar cheese	¼ cup	60 mL

Cut off any tough ends of asparagus. Lay spears in 5 quart (5 L) slow cooker.

Stir flour, salt and pepper together in saucepan. Whisk in evaporated milk gradually until no lumps remain. Heat and stir until boiling and thickened.

Stir in cheese to melt. Pour over asparagus. Cover. Cook on Low for 3 to 4 hours. If you like your asparagus crunchy, check for doneness at 2 to 2½ hours. Remove asparagus with slotted spoon. Serves 6.

1 serving: 71 Calories; 1.9 g Total Fat; 185 mg Sodium; 6 g Protein; 8 g Carbohydrate

Pictured on page 71.

RED CABBAGE

It does lose its brightness but keeps the good taste.

Small red cabbage, quartered, cored and thinly sliced (about 2 lbs., 900 g)	1	1
Chopped onion	1½ cups	375 mL
Medium cooking apples (such as McIntosh), peeled, cored and chopped	3	3
Brown sugar, packed	¼ cup	60 mL
Water	½ cup	125 mL
White vinegar	¼ cup	60 mL
Hard margarine (or butter), melted	1 tbsp.	15 mL
Salt	1 tsp.	5 mL
Pepper	¼ tsp.	1 mL

Place all 9 ingredients in 5 quart (5 L) slow cooker. Stir to coat all with liquid. Cover. Cook on Low for 5 to 6 hours or on High for 2½ to 3 hours. Makes 7 cups (1.75 L).

½ cup (125 mL): 64 Calories; 1.1 g Total Fat; 213 mg Sodium; 1 g Protein; 14 g Carbohydrate

Glazing just before serving gives this a hint of sweetness.

Small whole acorn squash	3	3
Water	¼ cup	60 mL
TOPPING		
Liquid honey	3 tbsp.	50 mL
Hard margarine (or butter), softened	2 tbsp.	30 mL
Salt	½ tsp.	2 mL
Pepper	⅛ tsp.	0.5 mL

Place squash in 5 quart (5 L) slow cooker. Pour water over top. Cover. Cook on Low for 8 hours.

Topping: Mix all 4 ingredients well. Cut each squash in half lengthwise. Scoop out seeds. Brush cavities and edges with honey mixture. Serves 6.

1 serving: 132 Calories; 4.3 g Total Fat; 279 mg Sodium; 3 g Protein; 24 g Carbohydrate; good source of Dietary Fiber

Pictured on page 107.

GLAZED CARROTS

These are best cooked on High to keep the great taste of carrot. Nicely glazed.

Peeled baby carrots	2 lbs.	900 g
Water	¼ cup	60 mL
Cornstarch	1 tbsp.	15 mL
Brown sugar, packed	½ cup	125 mL
Hard margarine (or butter), melted	1 tbsp.	15 mL

Place carrot in 3½ quart (3.5 L) slow cooker.

Stir water, cornstarch, brown sugar and margarine together in small bowl. Pour over carrot. Cover. Cook on High for 3 to 4 hours. Stir before serving. Makes 5 cups (1.25 L).

½ cup (125 mL): 95 Calories; 1.2 g Total Fat; 48 mg Sodium; 1 g Protein; 21 g Carbohydrate

CARROT ONION CASSEROLE

The slow cooking really brings out the carrot and onion flavors.

Diagonally sliced carrot	6 cups	1.5 L
Sliced onion	1½ cups	375 mL
Salt	½ tsp.	2 mL
Water	½ cup	125 mL
SAUCE		
All-purpose flour	1 tbsp.	15 mL
Salt, sprinkle		
Pepper, sprinkle		
Milk	½ cup	125 mL
Grated medium or sharp Cheddar cheese	½ cup	125 mL
TOPPING		
Hard margarine (or butter)	1 tbsp.	15 mL
Fine dry bread crumbs	¼ cup	60 mL

Place carrot, onion, salt and water in 3½ quart (3.5 L) slow cooker. Stir. Cover. Cook on High for 4 to 5 hours. Drain. Place in serving bowl.

Sauce: Stir flour, salt and pepper together in small saucepan. Whisk in milk gradually until no lumps remain. Heat and stir until boiling and thickened.

Add cheese. Stir to melt. Pour over vegetables. Stir.

Topping: Melt margarine in saucepan. Stir in bread crumbs. Heat and stir until browned. Sprinkle over vegetables before serving. Makes 6 cups (1.5 L).

½ cup (125 mL): 92 Calories; 3.1 g Total Fat; 177 mg Sodium; 3 g Protein; 14 g Carbohydrate

Pictured on page 17.

Paré Pointer

Patience is yours if you can count down before you blast off.

MEASUREMENT TABLES

Throughout this book measurements are given in Conventional and Metric measure. To compensate for differences between the two measurements due to rounding, a full metric measure is not always used. The cup used is the standard 8 fluid ounce. Temperature is given in degrees Fahrenheit and Celsius. Baking pan measurements are in inches and centimetres as well as quarts and litres. An exact metric conversion is given below as well as the working equivalent (Standard Measure).

OVEN TEMPERATURES

Fahrenheit (°F)	Celsius (°C)
175°	80°
200°	95°
225°	110°
250°	120°
275°	140°
300°	150°
325°	160°
350°	175°
375°	190°
400°	205°
425°	220°
450°	230°
475°	240°
500°	260°

SPOONS

Conventional Measure	Metric Exact Conversion Millilitre (mL)	Metric Standard Measure Millilitre (mL)
1/8 teaspoon (tsp.)	0.6 mL	0.5 mL
1/4 teaspoon (tsp.)	1.2 mL	1 mL
1/2 teaspoon (tsp.)	2.4 mL	2 mL
1 teaspoon (tsp.)	4.7 mL	5 mL
2 teaspoons (tsp.)	9.4 mL	10 mL
1 tablespoon (tbsp.)	14.2 mL	15 mL

CUPS

1/4 cup (4 tbsp.)	56.8 mL	60 mL
1/3 cup (51/3 tbsp.)	75.6 mL	75 mL
1/2 cup (8 tbsp.)	113.7 mL	125 mL
2/3 cup (102/3 tbsp.)	151.2 mL	150 mL
3/4 cup (12 tbsp.)	170.5 mL	175 mL
1 cup (16 tbsp.)	227.3 mL	250 mL
41/2 cups	1022.9 mL	1000 mL (1 L)

PANS

Conventional Inches	Metric Centimetres
8x8 inch	20x20 cm
9x9 inch	22x22 cm
9x13 inch	22x33 cm
10x15 inch	25x38 cm
11x17 inch	28x43 cm
8x2 inch round	20x5 cm
9x2 inch round	22x5 cm
10x41/2 inch tube	25x11 cm
8x4x3 inch loaf	20x10x7.5 cm
9x5x3 inch loaf	22x12.5x7.5 cm

DRY MEASUREMENTS

Conventional Measure Ounces (oz.)	Metric Exact Conversion Grams (g)	Metric Standard Measure Grams (g)
1 oz.	28.3 g	28 g
2 oz.	56.7 g	57 g
3 oz.	85.0 g	85 g
4 oz.	113.4 g	125 g
5 oz.	141.7 g	140 g
6 oz.	170.1 g	170 g
7 oz.	198.4 g	200 g
8 oz.	226.8 g	250 g
16 oz.	453.6 g	500 g
32 oz.	907.2 g	1000 g (1 kg)

CASSEROLES (Canada & Britain)

Standard Size Casserole	Exact Metric Measure
1 qt. (5 cups)	1.13 L
11/2 qts. (71/2 cups)	1.69 L
2 qts. (10 cups)	2.25 L
21/2 qts. (121/2 cups)	2.81 L
3 qts. (15 cups)	3.38 L
4 qts. (20 cups)	4.5 L
5 qts. (25 cups)	5.63 L

CASSEROLES (United States)

Standard Size Casserole	Exact Metric Measure
1 qt. (4 cups)	900 mL
11/2 qts. (6 cups)	1.35 L
2 qts. (8 cups)	1.8 L
21/2 qts. (10 cups)	2.25 L
3 qts. (12 cups)	2.7 L
4 qts. (16 cups)	3.6 L
5 qts. (20 cups)	4.5 L

INDEX

Company's Coming cookbooks are available at retail locations throughout Canada!

EXCLUSIVE mail order offer on next page

Buy any 2 cookbooks—choose a 3rd FREE of equal or less value than the lowest price paid.

Original Series — CA$15.99 Canada — US$12.99 USA & International

CODE		CODE		CODE	
SQ	150 Delicious Squares	BB	Breakfasts & Brunches	ASI	Asian Cooking
CA	Casseroles	SC	Slow Cooker Recipes	CB	The Cheese Book
MU	Muffins & More	ODM	One-Dish Meals	RC	The Rookie Cook
SA	Salads	ST	Starters	RHR	Rush-Hour Recipes
AP	Appetizers	SF	Stir-Fry	SW	Sweet Cravings
SS	Soups & Sandwiches	MAM	Make-Ahead Meals	YRG	Year-Round Grilling
CO	Cookies	PB	The Potato Book	GG	Garden Greens
PA	Pasta	CCLFC	Low-Fat Cooking	CHC	Chinese Cooking
BA	Barbecues	CCLFP	Low-Fat Pasta	PK	The Pork Book
PR	Preserves	CFK	Cook For Kids	RL	Recipes For Leftovers
CH	Chicken, Etc.	SCH	Stews, Chilies & Chowders		
KC	Kids Cooking	FD	Fondues		
CT	Cooking For Two	CCBE	The Beef Book		

Greatest Hits Series

CODE	CA$12.99 Canada US$9.99 USA & International
ITAL	Italian
MEX	Mexican

Lifestyle Series

CODE	CA$17.99 Canada US$15.99 USA & International
GR	Grilling
DC	Diabetic Cooking

CODE	CA$19.99 Canada US$15.99 USA & International
HC	Heart-Friendly Cooking
DDI	Diabetic Dinners **NEW** *March 1/04*

Most Loved Recipe Collection

CODE	CA$23.99 Canada US$19.99 USA & International
MLA	Most Loved Appetizers
MLMC	Most Loved Main Courses **NEW** *April 1/04*

Special Occasion Series

CODE	CA$20.99 Canada US$19.99 USA & International
GFK	Gifts from the Kitchen
CFS	Cooking for the Seasons

CODE	CA$22.99 Canada US$19.99 USA & International
WC	Weekend Cooking

CODE	CA$25.99 Canada US$22.99 USA & International
HFH	Home for the Holidays
DD	Decadent Desserts

Company's Coming
COOKBOOKS®

Company's Coming Publishing Limited
2311 – 96 Street
Edmonton, Alberta, Canada T6N 1G3
Tel: 780-450-6223 Fax: 780-450-1857
www.companyscoming.com

EXCLUSIVE Mail Order Offer
See previous page for list of cookbooks

Quantity	Code	Title	Price Each	Price Total
			$	$
		DON'T FORGET		
		to indicate your		
		FREE BOOK(S)		
		(see exclusive mail order		
		offer above)		
		please print		

TOTAL BOOKS (including FREE)	TOTAL BOOKS PURCHASED:	$

	International	Canada & USA
Plus Shipping & Handling (per destination)	$11.98 (one book)	$5.98 (one book)
Additional Books (including FREE books)	$ ($4.99 each)	$ ($1.99 each)
Sub-Total	$	$
Canadian residents add G.S.T.(7%)		$
TOTAL AMOUNT ENCLOSED	$	$

The Fine Print

☐ MasterCard   ☐ VISA

Expiry date

Account #

Name of cardholder

Cardholder's signature

Gift Giving

Shipping Address
Send the cookbooks listed above to:

Name:

Street:

City: Prov./State:

Country: Postal Code/Zip:

Tel: (   )

Email address:

☐ YES! Please send a catalogue

New February 1st, 2004

Company's Coming
Recipes For Leftovers

Jean Paré
ORIGINAL SERIES

Save time, effort and money by making the most of your leftovers! *Recipes For Leftovers* includes practical recipes for turning leftover dishes into tasty dishes your family will enjoy.

In this book:
- Chicken & Turkey
- Fish
- Ham
- Pork & Lamb
- Pasta, Potatoes & Rice
- Vegetables

Company's Coming
COOKBOOKS®

Quick
&
Easy
Recipes

Everyday
Ingredients

Canada's
most popular
cookbooks!

Complete your Original Series Collection!

- ❏ 150 Delicious Squares
- ❏ Casseroles
- ❏ Muffins & More
- ❏ Salads
- ❏ Appetizers
- ❏ Soups & Sandwiches
- ❏ Cookies
- ❏ Pasta
- ❏ Barbecues
- ❏ Preserves
- ❏ Chicken, Etc.
- ❏ Kids Cooking
- ❏ Cooking For Two
- ❏ Breakfasts & Brunches
- ❏ Slow Cooker Recipes
- ❏ One-Dish Meals
- ❏ Starters
- ❏ Stir-Fry
- ❏ Make-Ahead Meals
- ❏ The Potato Book
- ❏ Low-Fat Cooking
- ❏ Low-Fat Pasta
- ❏ Cook For Kids
- ❏ Stews, Chilies & Chowders
- ❏ Fondues
- ❏ The Beef Book
- ❏ Asian Cooking
- ❏ The Cheese Book
- ❏ The Rookie Cook
- ❏ Rush-Hour Recipes
- ❏ Sweet Cravings
- ❏ Year-Round Grilling
- ❏ Garden Greens
- ❏ Chinese Cooking
- ❏ The Pork Book
- ❏ Recipes For Leftovers

COLLECT ALL Company's Coming Series Cookbooks!

Greatest Hits Series
- ❏ Italian
- ❏ Mexican

Lifestyle Series
- ❏ Grilling
- ❏ Diabetic Cooking
- ❏ Heart-Friendly Cooking
- ❏ Diabetic Dinners
  NEW *March 1/04*

Most Loved Recipe Collection
- ❏ Most Loved Appetizers
- ❏ Most Loved Main Courses
  NEW *April 1/04*

Special Occasion Series
- ❏ Gifts from the Kitchen
- ❏ Cooking for the Seasons
- ❏ Home for the Holidays
- ❏ Weekend Cooking
- ❏ Decadent Desserts

Canada's most popular cookbooks!